The World we don't see

Mirza Yawar Baig

ISBN: 9781797934662

Table of Contents

Preface

Looking and seeing are as different as hearing and listening. One is a function of the organ. The other, a matter of the mind and heart. It indicates interest, awakening and joy. You may say that doesn't apply to every case. I will say that nothing applies to every case. But on the average, listening beats hearing and seeing beats looking every single time, joy or not.

This book is about seeing. Seeing with the heart because it's not the eyes that go blind but our hearts that can no longer see.

I've always made it a point to ensure that my heart remains intact and able to see. To ensure that, I go into the bush periodically and spend time in the forest. I usually go to places where there's no telephone and obviously no internet. The joy of disconnecting from these enslavers can't be expressed. It must be experienced. To the seriously intoxicated, it is painful to begin with. But stay away from them long enough, wake up to bird calls every morning, listen to the forest day and night and you'll feel the cares of the world fall away.

Most reluctantly, I return to my city life, waiting once again to go back to my life of seclusion. I've tried to share my experiences, thoughts and feelings I this book. But I strongly recommend that you get away, go into a forest, sit quietly under a tree and listen. Listen and see. And then ask your heart to explain.

I hope you'll enjoy reading this at least as much as I enjoyed living these moments.

Yawar Baig

We are living beings, not binary code

IN TODAY'S WORLD, one of the things that I am most conscious about is the need to connect with the land. In my case, that means forests. Urban living has ripped out the connection we all had with the earth and left us with a lifestyle which is deceptive and artificial. Millennials are addicted to tech gadgets, not to the sound of birdsong early in the morning. Many have never smelled the first rain on parched earth, a perfume which the Attars (perfume makers) of old captured in an Atar (perfume) called Atar-e-Gil or Mitti Atar. Many don't know the feel of good loamy soil in their hands or the pleasure of planting a tree and then watching it take root, grow and flower, over the weeks. For many eggs come from the grocery store, n=ot from chickens with a personality and clear likes and dislikes of places and people, which they don't hesitate to make known. I can go on but this will suffice. I believe it is critically important for us to change that and get people to smell the earth, listen to the forest and feel a sense of companionship with those who inhabit the earth with us. As we are headed into global warming and environmental destruction, I can't help but feel that this is because most of us don't even know what we are losing or what an unspoilt environment looks and feels like. What we don't understand, we fear and what we fear, we destroy.

All through my childhood and youth, 1960's & 70's, I spent as much time in the forests as I could which enabled me to indulge my deep and abiding interest in wildlife and ecology. I had three of the best teachers that one could hope for to learn jungle craft from. People who loved the forests, had a wealth of knowledge about them and had the patience and affection to convey it to a young boy. They were Capt. Nadir Tyabji, Nawab Nazir Yar Jung and my dear Uncle Rama (Venkat Rama Reddy). All were more than twenty years my senior but that has always been my situation, friends who are older and wiser from whom I learn all the time. I owe them a debt of gratitude and remember them with boundless respect and love. They invested countless hours in me for no material return and taught me lessons which fall into place to this day, fifty years later. It is a very rare privilege to have mentors like them and I am forever grateful.

From Nadir uncle I learnt to observe quietly without disturbing what I was looking at. I learnt from him the amazing variety of living beings that live in harmony with one another in a small little pond. I learnt a lot about birds, their nesting habits, their camouflage techniques and that the term, 'free as a bird' is a figment of the imagination. Birds are often so tied down to their environment, often a single species of tree, that if that tree dies, so does the bird. Out of this, I learnt to appreciate not one or two selected creatures but the whole spectrum of trees, insects, birds, reptiles and mammals that make up our environment. This was at a time when to get to the nearest pond with some undisturbed rocks and bush around it, took all of ten minutes walking.

I was able to appreciate the importance of not upsetting this balance and what happens when in our endless greed we thoughtlessly destroy our environment. I saw that pond, the rocks and scrub forest around it, listened to the cooing of doves in the trees, saw the jacana with her chicks skipping on the lily pads. I saw the mongoose come out of her den in the rocks and look at me, unafraid because she had seen me so often and knew that I posed no threat to her babies. I heard the cawing of crows and the endless chatter of sparrows. I saw the hoopoe swoop down from the sky onto a patch of grass and dig for worms with his sharp beak, raising his crown from time to time, to remind the world of who he is. Some years later when I returned to Hyderabad, I tried to visit that pond. I say tried to visit because to be able to visit, the object of your visit needs to be there. It wasn't. The rocks had been blasted to make concrete. The pond had been filled in, the trees cut, the grass ground underfoot into dust. The mongoose, the jacana, the doves and hoopoe, even the crows and sparrows, all gone, never to return. What I saw was a tar road, a concrete high-rise building with climate control (meaning, no windows) and the whir of traffic. Was that the worst of it or was it that there was nobody to mourn their passing?

From Nawab Nazir Yar Jung (we called him Nawabsab) I learnt the basics of self defence, shooting, training dogs and horses and jungle craft. He taught me how to train dogs for tracking, retrieving and guarding. I was learning from a man who had an international standing in his art and I was very conscious of it. What I was also learning in the process of training dogs and horses, which I was not conscious of then, was about myself, my strengths, weaknesses, fears, hopes and emotions. Dogs react to facial expressions and unconscious movements and mannerisms and their performance depends on the clarity with which a command is given. To the man, it may appear that the command is the word alone. But to the dog it is a combination of sound, expression and the slightest movement all together as one. So, if you are not conscious of yourself, then your dog will always be confused because your command comes across to him differently each time. Today, when I teach presentation skills or facilitate meetings I recall these lessons in self-awareness and the power of synchronizing yourself in thought, word and action. Dogs taught me how to deal with people.

Uncle Rama taught me more than I can possibly list here. He taught me the meaning of responsibility and accountability. He taught me to take care of myself in a hostile environment. He taught me to be at peace with the forest, to connect with the stars and to respect the animals we occasionally shot for the table. Hunting was not a sport. It was something you did only for necessity and with a sense of deep thankfulness for the fact that the animal gave its life for you. Hunting was a contest between man with his weak senses and a good rifle and the animal with his speed of response, his highly tuned senses, his intuition and his enormous knowledge of his environment. It was not only an equal contest but was usually in favor of the animal. That is when you played fair. This means that you tracked the animal on foot, in daylight. Not when you used a high-powered searchlight to blind it in the night and then did target practice. That I was taught, is the most despicable, dishonorable and shameless thing that you could do. And so, I never did it.

All these were ostensibly lessons in anything but work. But in reality, they were lessons in character building, life skills, influencing, social dynamics, self-awareness and understanding which have stood me in very good stead all through my life and which are the backbone of my profession of leadership training.

I became very skilled in jungle craft and could stalk game in silence over long distances. I could camouflage myself and stay hidden and unobserved and walk a trail and tell the signs of creatures that had walked that path ahead of me. The more I knew about an animal the more likely I was to be able to track it down and shoot it. So, I studied, talked to people who were knowledgeable, and observed. My observation became very good and so did my ability to listen to and analyze sounds. In the Indian forests, home to large and potentially dangerous mammals, this knowledge can often mean the difference between life and death. As I learned more about forests, I enjoyed my time in the forests even more and looked forward to the holidays when I would get on a bus and travel to Nirmal, change buses for Khanapur and Pembi and then walk the last four kilometers to Sethpalli.

Uncle Rama was like a father to me and he would give me a royal welcome. He used to call me Nawab and treated me like a king. That I was a fifteen-year-old schoolboy meant nothing to him. To him I was his friend, who he treated as an equal. As soon as I arrived, covered in dust, I would go off to the well at the edge of the Tamarind trees, which shaded the house on the riverbank. There I would stand in my underwear and one of the farm workers (usually Shivaiyya, my Gond tracker friend) would draw water in a bucket from the well and pour it over my head. Lots of soap, more water flooded over my head, and I would be clean as two whistles. Dressed in a lungi and banyan, I would sit on the charpoy opposite Uncle Rama under one of the Tamarind trees and he would tell me all that had happened since my last visit. While this was going on, his cook would bring a huge bowl of fried Chital meat and I would eat and listen to him. I had a vast capacity for eating meat and tender Chital was my absolute favorite. Uncle Rama knew that I was Muslim and would not eat anything not slaughtered in the Islamic way. So, he used to take one of his Muslim workers, Noorullah, with him when he went hunting. Once the animal was down, Noorullah would go and slaughter it by cutting the throat and saying: Bismillahi Allahu Akbar. Such was the consideration we were taught to observe for one another.

I loved jungles. I loved hunting and I loved Uncle Rama above all else. So, every holiday I would go off to Sethpalli. Sometimes Uncle Rama would be in town (Hyderabad) at the time my holidays were about to begin. He would call and say, "Kya Nawab, chalna hai?" And off we went. He had a BSA motorcycle (350 cc). He would ride with a .12 bore shotgun slung across his chest and a bandolier of cartridges and I would ride behind him with a .22 bore rifle slung across my back.

How can I describe the excitement as I rode behind Uncle Rama with the wind in my face? Those were the days before helmets were invented; before there were any Naxalites in those forests and before it became illegal to hunt. So off we would go from Hyderabad to Sethpalli, via Nirmal and Khanapur. All names that conjure up wonderful memories of a childhood that today no child can even dream of. This is the price we have paid for what we like to call 'development'.

As we went along, Uncle Rama would stop by a road side water tank. These tanks were an integral part of the irrigation network of Telangana, which does not see too much rain. Every village had its tank. When maintained, they harvested rain water, enhanced the water table in the village and provided water to irrigate the fields so that in most years people were able to harvest two crops. The tanks had fish and attracted water birds, both of which added to the villager's diet. And they were very beautiful. Today they have been allowed to silt up. The dams are ruined. The entire irrigation system has been allowed to collapse with nothing else to replace it. Some of them have been encroached upon and people have built houses and shops on the tank bed, which is illegal of course. Alas, when the grease hits the palm in India, anything is possible. The result is drought, uncultivated lands and in years when the monsoon fails, starvation, and farmer suicides.

Uncle Rama would park his motorcycle by the roadside and we would get off, un-sling the guns and sneak up the embankment of the nearby water tank. There, sure enough, we would find, Brahminy, Pollard, Comb (Nakta) ducks, or Teals. All floating in the reeds and feeding in the shallows. Uncle Rama was a master tracker and I learnt from him. We would crawl along the bank, just below the top, careful not to show a silhouette and when we were in range, I would fire first and he would take the flying shots as the ducks rose in flight. Usually, we would get our dinner before we reached home. We would arrive at the farm with the motorcycle festooned with ducks on either side.

The villagers also hunt ducks. The difference is they do it without firearms. In this part of the world, they don't even have any bows and arrows, catapults, or any other throwing weapons. What they do is to take a round pot with a mouth big enough for the head of the hunter to go through and make two holes in it to see through. They then seal the holes and the mouth of the pot and float it among the reeds where ducks take shelter in the night. After a couple of days, the ducks get used to seeing the pot in their midst. Then on a moonless night, the hunter creeps up quietly, enters the water and inserts his head into the pot, making sure that his body is completely submerged. He looks through the holes in the pot and breathes the air trapped in the pot. To the ducks, it is still the same pot floating among the reeds. Then the hunter very quietly and gently approaches a duck and grabs its legs under the water, yanking it down below the surface. Done expertly, the duck simply disappears without trace. The man transfers the duck to his other hand and then approaches the next duck to yank it to its watery end. The only thing limiting him is the number of duck legs he can hold in one hand. On a good day, getting five or six ducks is not difficult. Some hunters wear a belt to which they attach all underwater ducks which considerably increases their game bag. These ducks were a valuable addition of protein in their diet as well as a means of earning some money. Human ingenuity is truly the best resource we have.

Khanapur was the first watering hole. The first serious one that is. We would stop for tea at one of the many road-side Dhabas and Uncle Rama would have fun talking to the owner in fluent Telugu only to see the look of total surprise on his face. Uncle Rama, due to his English mother, was himself white with blond hair. So, people naturally took him to be British. And when he spoke colloquial Telugu and Urdu fluently, they were shocked.

In Khanapur we would stop at his house which he never actually finished building. He'd started it in the hope that his family would live there with him. But his wife, a wonderful, cultured lady did not fancy the village life, so he never finished the house. It was still livable though and we would stop there for lunch. After lunch he would pull out a big bottle with a viscous liquid that looked like old engine oil. What it contained was the most delicious honey that I have ever eaten. Fifty years later that statement still holds true. It was so black and viscous because it was so old and high in sugar content that it was practically solid. This honey with butter was the dessert...blisssssssssssssssssssssss, which was followed by two hours of sound sleep. The idea was to wait for the heat of the afternoon to lessen before travelling. In summer the temperatures there would be in the high forties (north of 115 F), even though we were in the middle of the forest. To travel in that heat (especially on a motorcycle) was a good way to get sunstroke. All life comes to a standstill at midday and then people start to move again once the sun is on its way to rising in America.

In the evening, after a cup of tea we would leave for Sethpalli, our final destination, sometimes in the Jeep that Uncle Rama used to cache in Khanapur, or on the motorbike. This drive was the most exciting part of the whole trip as the road went through thick forests. Much of it teak plantations. Some original forest. A lot of bamboo thickets and Ber bushes; favorite haunts of wildlife ranging from Jungle Fowl who eat the berries and seed, to Gaur which graze on tender bamboo shoots to tigers who like to lie up in the shade of the bamboo which is not deciduous and remains green in the summer. A good place to look for tigers is bamboo bordering any small creek or even a dry stream bed (Nalla). Tigers love to lie in the relatively cool sand or in the water all through the heat of the day, shaded from the sun and prying eyes by the thick bamboo fronds.

The semi-deciduous forests of the Satpura Range are relatively open without much undergrowth. One of the reasons for this is also the annual burning that happens even though it is illegal. Shepherds and others set fire to the undergrowth and this burns off all the dry leaves on the forest floor causing minor damage to the large trees. That leaves the place open for the growth of new grass and shrubs. Deer and Gaur love this new growth as also the ash from the burnt logs which they come to eat. The ash is also excellent manure for the new growth and it grows lush and thick. As we drove through the evening, rapidly turning to night, we would often see herds of Chital, Nilgai, the occasional Sambar (they usually start moving much later after moonset) and Gaur lying or feeding in the open forest glades. Most were so used to the sound of traffic that as long as the vehicle was moving, they would simply look up to see what it was and then continue on with whatever they were doing. But if the vehicle stopped, they would immediately be alarmed and start to move away.

Uncle Rama used these trips to teach me from his vast knowledge of jungle lore. I learnt to distinguish between a male and female animal. To recognize one that was pregnant or nursing. To recognize their different moods and what the calls meant. Some raised in alarm, the belling of a Sambar; the barking of the Cheetal, hooting of the Langur sentinel who sees the danger before anyone else and on whose vigilance, they all depend. I learnt the meaning of a deer staring in concentration at one thicket and then stamping his fore hoof a couple of times before barking alarm. By listening to the belling of a Sambar in the night, I learnt to tell which direction he was looking in and how far he was from me. In forests that had many tigers and leopards, this was a very useful skill indeed.

I learnt to read tracks and tell whether the animal was running or walking, the number of animals in the herd that had crossed the stream bed. I learnt to tell what they had been eating by examining their dung. I learnt the difference in the shape of the dung pellets which is the signature of the animal. So many things to learn. I learnt how to stalk deer until I got close enough to get a killing shot. I learnt where on the body to aim and shoot so that the animal dies instantly and painlessly. I learnt. I learnt. I learnt. And I loved every minute of it.

The big challenge we have today is to teach our children these lessons and help them to connect to the earth, to its inhabitants and to each other. We are living beings, not binary code. The earth is not at our mercy but waits and watches to see what we do. Then it will do what it has done in the past, to protect what is beneficial and to heal itself by ridding itself of that which is harmful. Our call to define ourselves.

World before plastics

First a disclaimer: Nostalgia alert: Not everything old is or was good. Not everything new is or was bad. But nostalgia feels so good. So, enjoy and keep the salt handy.

In the world before plastics, glasses were made of glass, or copper or silver and water tasted better in them. Bottles were transparent glass or opaque ceramic. But both were breakable and did. Plates were ceramic beautifully painted. Also breakable and did. We also had steel plates which didn't break but were less classy. Buckets and tubs were unbreakable, made of copper or galvanized iron and made a loud clang when you put them down and dropped the handle. So you were careful to put the handle down gently.

Shopping bags were cloth, washed and reused until they wore out and then served as dish and polishing cloths until they vanished. Chairs were wooden or metal – some foldable, some not. All heavy and unstackable. So when plastic bottles, plates, cups, buckets and tubs and above all plastic bags came to be, we were thrilled out of our minds. Transparent like glass but doesn't break? Buckets and tubs lifting which didn't break your back? Chairs that could be stacked and put away when you didn't need them? Shopping bags that you could print your label on and which the customer could use for other things or simply throw away? No need to wash and dry and reuse. Truly a vision of convenience heaven.

Beds were wooden cots without springs with cotton mattresses on them. Every year a man would come with an instrument that resembled a great bow and would be shut into a room with all mattresses. He would unstitch one side, pull out the cotton, prong it with his bow until it was fluffy once again and then stuff it back into the mattress. When you entered the room to give the man a cup of tea, you had to look for him in the white cloud of cotton fluff and dust that he generated. The drumming sound of him working was like an out of tune sitar. What it did to his lungs breathing in the cotton fluff, is not something that either he or we were conscious of but thanks to spring-less beds and firm mattresses we didn't have backaches. PUF was unheard of. Foam was on soaps, not mattresses. And soaps were in the bathroom, not on TV. There was no TV.

Our home had resident wildlife - sparrows in the rafters making an infernal din every morning belligerently defending their nesting sites from intruders. In Urdu they are very aptly called Khana Chidiya (Khanchudi in Deccani) - house bird. Their feathers and at nesting time, all the grass and other tidbits they brought and then allowed to fall - they are incredibly messy nest builders - meant that the house had to be swept twice or three times a day. Occasionally a sparrow would get brained by a lazily rotating fan because they never seemed to realize that trying to perch on a moving fan was a bad idea. We would pick up the dazed bird and revive it and put it on a window sill so that it could fly away when it wished. It never occurred to us to de-sparrow the house. Sweeping was preferable to an aseptic house devoid of the chirping of the sparrow. Today with all the concrete and glass and pesticide sprays in the fields, sparrows are gone.

Municipal water came when it came so everyone had storage tanks in bathrooms. If those ran out there was the Bi-hish-ti (literally: man from heaven) who came with a leather sack slung over his shoulder and topped up the tank. More usually he would water the garden and simply sprinkle water in the yard after sunset to cool the place down before our cots would be set out for us to sleep under the stars all through summer. Those who didn't have gardens had terraces or flat roofs used for the same purpose. How did it feel to lie in bed and look at the moon and stars through your mosquito net, secure in the thought that your house was not being burgled while you slept? I don't think I can even tell you to try it out today. The world before plastics was different.

In that world, we had no computers but we had time. We had no TV but we had friends. We had no cell phones but we spoke to people face to face. Conversation was an art, taught and learnt and grunts didn't substitute for words. Language had value and was acquired and husbanded – new words tried out to see how they worked – phrases repeated, shared and appreciated. Poetry was an actual form of self-expression that underlined the thought and the ability to quote the right couplet at the right time was a mark of a person's education. Conversation didn't simply revolve around politics or controversial matters but we talked about thought leaders, exemplars of our past and shared their thoughts and writings, often verbatim – memorizing and quoting them being a sign of our own worth. An hour or two passed in this way, drinking tea and reciting poetry and marveling at the turn of phrase, expressing thoughts that touched the heart was something to be looked forward to and back on with great pleasure.

We worked in the home or for our families for love or duty but never for money. We were never offered money and would have considered it an insult to be offered payment for doing something for our family members, no matter how distant. The concept of paying children to work in the home was unheard of and considered deplorable. Money was called 'dirt on the hands' – we dirtied our hands for the experience. The dirt came as a result – we didn't work for it. Mentioning what anything cost, what anybody earned or what anyone had spent on a gift, meal or any other form of hospitality was considered insulting and crass. Hospitality was a value, not an industry. The guest was someone you invited home to a meal. To take him to a restaurant was considered a lapse in the standard of hospitality. Even if you did it, it was done under duress. Never as a choice. If some family member informed us that he or she was arriving from another city, it was the standard for us to meet them at the station and bring them home.

I will never forget the picture of my great-uncle Nawab Ruknuddin Ahmed standing on the platform on Chennai station with garlands when I arrived there in 1985 with my newly wedded wife Samina. He was staying with his daughter, Aunty Jahanara, who we would be transiting with on our way to the tea gardens where I worked. Even though it was not his home that we were going to, Mamujaan honored us by personally receiving us at the station. But then what am I saying? How can the daughter's home not be his home? Just as my aunt's home was my home. We learnt from the actions of our elders.Tradition was to keep those memories alive – not only by talking about them, but by emulating the actions. For a family member to stay in a hotel instead of at home with us, was an insult to our honor. The thought that elderly parents could be sent away to a 'home' was unimaginable. Home was where we lived – not some place to shunt old inconvenient elders to, to be taken care of by strangers. They were our elders. We remembered what they did for us when we were little. To do the same for them, was not only our duty but not even something we considered remarkable.

In that world we played real games on real earth not virtual games on a gadget. We ran, sweated, yelled ourselves hoarse, tore our shirts, fell down, skinned our knees, got covered with dust and when it was raining with mud and considered all this as having a whale of a time. In these games we learned leadership, sharing, standing up for our friends, being done in by those we trusted and learnt lessons from all of them. We learned to work as a team, strategize and see the result of that strategy. We stood up for each other, never reneged on our friends, even when we sometimes had to pay the price for that loyalty. We settled with our friend in private but stood by his side in public. You didn't turn your back on your friends. It was as simple as that. It didn't matter to us what the color, religion or social status of the friend was. It didn't matter what car he drove because we all rode bicycles. It didn't matter what brand of clothing he wore because we all had clothes custom tailored by the Darzee (tailor) in our Muhalla (neighborhood). Bell bottoms were in fashion and we wore them. So were pointed shoes, and Brylcream in the hair. It didn't matter whether the friend was rich or poor because at the end of a good football game, we all looked the same – the color of mud. It didn't matter if he was tall or short, handsome or ugly. What mattered was that he was my friend. That was all.

In that world manners were everything. Manners meant that you showed respect to elders by greeting them first and standing up for them. By anticipating their needs and running to fulfill them. Manners meant that if an elder had to carry a chair to a place where he wanted to sit, it was an insult to you as the youngster who stood by and watched. Manners meant that you spoke politely after asking permission and listened more than you spoke. 'That is why you have been given two ears and one mouth' – we were told. Manners meant that when guests came home you served them, not servants. That you were in the middle of studying for your exam meant nothing. Guests were more important than exams. When the guests left you went back to studying and still got straight A's. No compromising on results.

In that world, we read books. Not occasionally but every single day. We had our favorite authors but we still had to read the classics mandatorily. Books were (and still are) our best friends, opening doors into worlds unexplored. We saw the scenes as we read about them, laughed with the actors in those stories, shared their joys and sorrows.

Books opened for us doors into the hearts and lives of the writers and their times walking through which we discovered ourselves. We read everything. J.R.R Tolkien, Ayn Rand, Alvin Toffler, Iqbal, Ghalib, Ibn Al Qayyim, Louis L'amour, George Orwell, Romila Thapar, James Herriot, Gerald Durrell, John Steinbeck, Munshi Premchand, Jakata Tales and many others, all spoke to us. They influenced us and shaped our thoughts and values and taught us to question, critically analyze and choose intelligently. Above all they taught us that we are not unique or more special than anyone else. That others also cry tears and laugh their way through difficulties and that in many cases our worst complaints are the dreams of others. We read and we learnt to write. We saw and we learnt to show by drawing vividly colored pictures with words. We dreamt and learnt to deal with the reality that some dreams are simply that – dreams. But that even the most unrealizable of them, opens vistas to that which might have been and leads to that which can become a reality. We learnt the value of philosophy and the solace it gives to a sore heart. We learnt to choose – sometimes painfully – but learnt the lesson that we could and must make choices. Sitting on the fence invariably gives you a sore crotch.

We had never heard of recycling but we always wore clothes that had graced the bottoms of our elder siblings. We used and reused them until the thing simply fell apart. Only then did we get anything new. Clothes covered our bodies, not our egos. Manners, not possessions were our statement. Not to say that we were always good mannered – one of the things we prided ourselves on was the ability to describe another's ancestry in colorful terms for ten minutes without repeating ourselves. A skill that comes in handy when one needs to de-stress. The secret is to do it alone facing a wall. Otherwise it increases stress levels instead of de-stressing.

Since we didn't have copy paste or auto correct, we learned spelling and wrote clearly in longhand. Ah! The joy of the feel of a fountain pen gliding smoothly across the page – these were the days before ball pens came into being. You chose your pen depending on the width of the nib. Sat with an inkpot and medicine dropper, filling the pen. Then screwed the top back on and carefully wiped the residual ink on your head and you were good to go. We wrote letters not only to give news but poured out our thoughts and feelings. Sometimes you would get a letter with a circle around a suspicious stain labelled 'tear'. Then we waited days and sometimes weeks before we got a reply.

We couldn't see the face, didn't get instant responses and had to struggle with translating emotion into words – so we learned to write properly. Our vocabulary was a lot more than, 'Ugh!, gr8, Like, youknowwhaimean? LOL. We didn't explore – we checked. We didn't reach out – we contacted. We didn't try to reach – we reached. We used shorthand to take notes and short forms only for telegrams. We learnt to imagine, anticipate and adjust. We learned patience and we learned to write legibly because the addressee had to read what we wrote. We learned to write concisely because we didn't want the reader to get bored and throw the letter away. We learned to write correctly and grammatically because not to do so was a sign of ignorance and a poor education. It still is.

In this world without instant coffee or tea bags we learnt the value of process – warm the tea pot before you pour in the hot water – and the reward of a properly done job – drink a cup of freshly ground coffee and you'll see what I mean. And the lesson that everything had a use – used tea leaves are excellent mulch for roses. Drinking tea was also about demonstrating upbringing – hold the cup by its handle between three finger and thumb with the little finger (pinky) sticking out and you don't slurp or blow on the tea to cool it. And god forbid, never slurp it out of the saucer. Not to say that doesn't have it's own pleasure but you didn't do it.

Not that everything in the plastic-less world was hunky dory — we had power cuts or to put it more correctly, we were delightfully surprised when we had power. But we had candles and lamps. We had no cooking gas and so our rotis came with a wood smoke flavor. Corn was always on the cob, roasted on live coals, rubbed with half a lemon dipped in salt and eaten hot. What all this cooking on wood did to the forests is another story. We had no refrigerators so we gave away all leftovers and always ate fresh. Milk would be stored overnight in what was called a Hawadaan (literally: air container) — a cupboard with a wooden frame and mesh sides. If it still turned we converted it either into a sweet or into ghee. As I said, we recycled out of necessity and it was very enjoyable.

My generation is a generation that straddles times and change. We have seen more fundamental change than both our predecessors and successors and we love it.

Grass Hills

THE ANAMALLAI HILLS are a ridge that is between three thousand five hundred to six thousand feet high and goes like the backbone of an elephant right down the Western side of India to the tip of the subcontinent. Even though it is not called by this name all along this journey and the name changes to High Range in Munnar and then other names, but it is the same range of mountains...all a part of the Western Ghats.

From Valparai Taluk, where the tea plantations of the Anamallais are and where I lived for seven years, there is a clear section of the ridge that goes all the way to Munnar in Kerala. These are the famous Grass Hills.

They are called Grass Hills because the hilltops are covered with tough tussocky grass which looks like a beautiful lawn from a distance but is very tough to walk through. The closest that I have seen to these are the Moors of Northumberland in England and Scottish Highlands. The land is very acidic and unable to grow anything else. The local Forest Department in its usual ham-handed way decided in the early 80's to plant Eucalyptus trees and convert the Grass Hills into money making machines. Nobody of course thought to ask the most logical question, "Why is it that if this land could grow trees, there is not a single tree to be seen?" But many millions of rupees and many thousands of man-hours later they learnt the lesson the hard way that these hills will grow nothing but the grass that's on them. In the grass are also some other small shrubs that are resistant to the wind and cold of the hilltops, which once in a year put forth the most beautiful flowers. I am not enough of a botanist to know all the names, but one of these flowers is famous and gives its name to the hills, Nilgiri – Blue Mountains.

I quote from a website dedicated to the flower: http://kurinji.in/kurinji.html

Neelakurinji (Strobilanthes kunthiana) is a shrub that used to grow abundantly in the shola grasslands of Western Ghats in India. The Nilgiris, which literally means the blue mountains, got its name from the purplish-blue flowers of Neelakurinji that blossoms gregariously once in 12 years. Once they used to cover the entire Nilgiris like a carpet during its flowering season. However, now plantations and dwellings occupy much of their habitat. Neelakurinji is the best known of a genus whose members have flowering cycles ranging from one to 16 years. It belongs to the family of Acanthaceae. The genus has more than 500 species, of which at least 56 occur in India. Besides the Western Ghats, Neelakurinji is seen in the Shevroys in the Eastern Ghats. It occurs at an altitude of 1300 to 2400 metres. The plant is usually 30 to 60 centimeters high on the hills. They can, however, grow well beyond 180 cm under congenial conditions at lower elevations. Plants that bloom at long intervals like Kurinji are called Plietesials.

The valleys are thickly forested often with little streams and waterfalls in them. These are called 'Shola' forests in Tamil. The Shola vegetation is peculiar to this habitat and is not found lower down. The trees have thick gnarled trunks, leathery leaves and grow densely together. This means that below them there is no undergrowth and creates a microclimate that is very cool, even cold. The streams flowing in the Sholas add moisture and this encourages the growth of moss, lichens and orchids and in the higher reaches, Rhododendrons. Philodendrons of many kinds are found in plenty, using the tree trunks to pull themselves upwards in the never-ending struggle for light.

Walking under the trees in the Shola forests is an experience that is impossible to describe but which once lived is never forgotten. Your footing is very uneven and slippery and so you must walk carefully. The ground is soft and damp and usually inclined, so you have one foot higher than the other as you walk. Not very conducive to long walks. But as you walk, suddenly you hear a rustle and a loud cackle and you see the fast disappearing tail feathers of a Jungle Cock and his harem, who were busily feeding on seeds and insects until you disturbed their breakfast. At this altitude in South India, it is the Grey Jungle Fowl that you will see. The females, as in the case of many birds, are a plain brown, their beauty lying only in the eyes of the beholding roosters. However, the males are flamboyant (takes more to attract a woman, I guess) with literally fluorescent, scintillating colored feathers, especially on the neck, which we call the hackle. These feathers shine and change color depending on the angle of the sunlight. The head is topped by a blood-red comb and the tail is a flowing graceful postscript to the whole story of the Grey Jungle Fowl. Just to see them move is a joy. Having extolled their virtues, let me add that they are very good eating, though a lot more gamey than the farmed free range chickens. The hackle makes extremely good flies for fly fishing and a couple of hackle feathers in a hat look very attractive indeed. However, farm chickens are easier to get and the hackle looks far nicer on the neck of the rooster, so leave them alone and shoot only with your camera.

Another delightful inhabitant of the Shola forests is the Malabar Whistling Thrush – also called the Whistling Schoolboy bird. It is a gorgeous blue-black bird, slightly larger than a Myna (the size of a Starling) and whistles just like we do. It is most vocal in the early mornings and late evenings and is an absolute delight to listen to. There was a pair that used to nest in a thick vine of Golden Showers which overhung the veranda roof of my bungalow on Lower Sheikalmudi Estate, and it was wonderful to open your eyes every morning to the whistling of the beautiful bird. Grass Hill Shola forests have more than their fair share of these birds and you can hear them as you walk along the side of the Sholas, picking your way through the tussocks of grass.

Snakes are around, especially at lower elevations, so keeping an eye open and wearing leather walking shoes is a good idea. In the stream of light that is let in because of the death of one of the trees in the Shola, you will find lush growth of grass, other vegetation, and sometimes an explosion of flowers. These sunny patches are also ideal places to look for the Muntjac antelope, also called Barking Deer. Its alarm call sounds like the bark of a dog, thus the name. When a Barking Deer is calling, almost always it means that he is looking at a leopard or tiger on the prowl and is warning all those who can understand the call to be on their guard. The Sambar is a more reliable sentinel for this warning, but the Muntjac is not too bad either. It's only that the

Muntjac is skittish and sometimes calls even when he is imagining one of the major predators.

The Shola forests of Grass Hills are ideal habitat for both predator and prey species. The forests impartially shelter leopards, tigers, wild boar, Muntjac, and Sambar. The thick shade hides the hunters and helps the hunted to escape. Depending of course on who sees whom first. Grass Hills and that entire ridge is also home to the Nilgiri Tahr (mistakenly called Ibex). These mountain goats live on the rocks walking up and jumping down from one invisible fold in the rock to another sometimes to get away from predators but often just for the fun of it. Their main predator is the leopard and they retreat to the inaccessible vertical ridges in the night to rest in relative safety.

The Grass Hills are also home to elephants and it is amazing to see how these huge animals negotiate steep ridges. First of all, they follow the easiest gradients as they go to the top. Many a savvy road engineer in these parts has simply widened an old elephant track to convert it into a motorable road, saving himself some arduous surveying. Then when they reach the top and have to actually negotiate the ridge, they walk in single file, each holding the tail of the one before it. And as they climb over the ridge, the one behind gives the one ahead a push as he needs it. On the way down they do it more simply – they sit down, keep their forelegs extended before them to act as speed breakers, and toboggan down the slope on their behinds.

As you climb up from Akkamalai Estate in the Anamallais after walking about 14 kilometers you eventually come upon a substantial stream. In the 70's and 80's it used to be stocked with Brown Trout. Check dams were built to make shallow pools and maintained by enthusiastic planters from nearby estates (Mr. Basith Khan of Tea Estates India was one) so that the level of water in the pools did not fall too low. These pools are important for the trout to feed and make good places to fish for them.

The check dams and the little pools they created became good drinking places for Gaur, Sambar, and elephant. While Sambar do not do any damage to the dam, Gaur and elephant sometimes inadvertently broke the dam and the water would drain away. This was disastrous for the fish, which would either be stranded or in the case of the young fry, would become easy prey for the many Kingfishers in the area. So, these dams had to be regularly maintained. Given that maintenance, the Grass Hills stream provided some excellent fly fishing in an ambience that simply can't be equaled. Where else in the world could you imagine being able to watch a herd of elephants or a lone Sambar while you were standing on the bank of the stream casting your fly? I won't talk about what the sight does to your casting because that is something that you have to experience.

The APA (Anamallai Planter's Association) had built a cottage at one point, called the Grass Hills Hut. It was a substantial two-bedroom cottage with a small veranda and an elephant trench all around. There was a flimsy bridge made of planks that you had to walk across to get inside. This was essential because without it elephants would try to re-engineer the hut; something which they did manage to do on a couple of occasions. It then fell into disuse and later the Forest

Department took it over and has now constructed a big concrete structure in its place at a huge cost, totally incongruous and sticking out like a sore thumb. But then how else can you spend public money if not in such obvious ways?

I used to go to Grass Hills as often as I could with my two companions, the Raman brothers. They were cousins and had the same name. We would leave my motorcycle in the garage of the Assistant Manager of Akkamalai Estate – it didn't matter if you knew the person or not. It was our code of hospitality that at such places your house was open to anyone who needed help. If someone wanted to park a car or motorcycle or needed some petrol or a cup of tea, he only had to ask and it was all provided with a smile. As I mentioned the distance to the APA Hut is about fourteen kilometers. If you don't take the road and instead walk up the hillside it is a couple of kilometers shorter, but you need a lot of stamina for the climb. The climb is steep, the elevation (six thousand feet) takes its toll especially if you are not used to it – as I discovered when I went to the Grass Hills in 2007 after a gap of twenty years. The footing is very rough and uncertain as the tough tussocky grass grows in clumps and you have to find your way between clumps. If it has been raining, then almost every single blade of grass will have a leech or two on it and you are more than likely to be viewed as manna from heaven by them. But if you can overcome the effort and the bloodshed then you are rewarded with some of the most spectacular views that you could ever imagine. The road is simpler and easier but like all simpler and easier tasks, less rewarding.

On one occasion the Raman brothers and I decided to walk up to a high ridge, which has some caves. When we eventually reached there, we discovered that there was a whole field of marijuana being cultivated in the valley behind the ridge and the cave was the living quarters of the farmers. In the middle was the cooking fire with their bedding stacked neatly in the corners. In one corner, there were wires to make snares for small game. Come to think of it, it was a very nice place to live with spectacular views, a stream of clear, cold water to drink from, a waterfall of ice cold water to shower under if you like that kind of thing, dry and warm accommodation, fresh meat, and safety from the long arm of the law. And if the arm did get extended this far, it was sent away with a handful of money. The occupants of the cave were not present when we reached there, which was probably a good thing for us.

We descended the ridge and made our way to the APA Hut. There the Raman brothers got busy with the cooking of our evening meal, the makings of which we had carried with us while I went downstream with my rod to catch a fish or two for the pot. To my disappointment, the check-dams had been broken by elephants and the pools had been drained and so there were no fish to catch except some very small fingerlings which were not worth the effort. But that didn't detract from the wonderful view of the sun going down behind the high ridge leaving behind an orange glow long after it had disappeared. I sat there until Raman the Elder came to call me. We ate our meal together and I got into my sleeping bag while the Ramans had their last smoke for the day before turning in. There was no need for a watch as we were surrounded by a trench around the hut. There is no danger in sleeping in the wild except from men with evil intentions.

Grass Hills is very cold at night so a good sleeping bag is essential. It is a very rare pleasure to be able to lie in your sleeping bag and listen to the sound of silence, broken occasionally by the call of the hunter or the unlucky hunted as it ends its life. Then there is the hooting of the owl and the occasional moan of the tiger. But for the most part the night at that elevation is silent. As the sky lightens, the precursor of dawn, I hear stirring in the kitchen where the Ramans made their bed. Social barriers (I was the manager) remain despite my every attempt at destroying them. But the fact that I don't practice them gets me loyalty that transcends time.

When I visited the Anamallais in 2007, one of the things I did was to revisit Grass Hills with my friends, the Ramans. They were as eager to go there again as I was. This time we didn't spend a night in the hut, but we did the walk up the hill, a source of great satisfaction and achievement for us all as we were still able to do it, despite being twenty years older. Almost nothing has changed in Grass Hills, mainly because the road is unmotorable and people are too lazy to do the climb. So, it remains relatively untouched. We did see a dozen forest guards with backpacks walking back from the Forest Department Cottage, which is what the APA Hut has been transformed into. What they are doing there in those numbers, I have no clue. But I hope it is something for the preservation of that wonderful habitat.

The Anamallais in general and the Grass Hills in particular are surely one of the most beautiful places on earth. I was privileged to live there and visit the Grass Hills on many occasions. I hope those who live there today feel equally privileged to do so and make the effort to leave these places alone and undisturbed. Going by what I saw when I was there last, I must say that I was not reassured.

An opportunity is what you create

I WAS IN the Anamallais, just married a few months and a lowly Assistant Manager in Lower Sheikalmudi Estate. My wife and I lived in the 'haunted' bungalow near the tennis court and I was busy trying to make a career and stand out in a fiercely competitive environment. I loved my life as a planter, which had all the requirements for heaven on earth as I conceptualized it. It was almost entirely outdoors. Walking up and down hills along forest boundaries with the certainty of seeing at least three or four species of mammals and countless birds, was not just possible but it was what I was being paid for. I can still hear the joyful cacophony of the birds, which I would hear every morning as I rode my bike or walked along the fire line that was the boundary between the tea and the forest. I know how to make sense of the sounds, to identify the sounds and distinguish the alarm call from the political argument. The political argument was of little interest to me, but the alarm call could mean the difference between being a spectator and a meal.

The Anamallais rain forest are home to tiger, leopard, bear, elephant, gaur, sambhar, barking deer, mouse deer, king cobra and many other snakes and langur and lion-tailed macaque. This is by no means an exhaustive list but one of some of the species that one could expect to encounter on a walk on any given day and all Sundays. The rain forest is too thick to walk through. Also, it is home to poisonous nettles called Anaimarti which if you rub against it in your foolish attempt to walk through the forest, creates an extremely painful reaction with swollen lymph nodes, high fever, violent rash and if you are very allergic to it and don't get treatment, even death. Add to this the incidence of leeches in uncounted numbers whose presence on your body you only discover when you have emerged from the forest and step into the shower and wonder why the water is so red. That is the color of your blood as it flows freely from the number of leech bites you returned with. Leeches are hematologists and inject heparin into the small wound they make as they bite you. That ensures that your blood doesn't clog and stop flowing. Then the leech attaches itself to the wound and simply fills up like a balloon with your blood. Once it is filled, it simply drops off. It you try to pull it out, it rips out and leaves its mouth parts in the wound to fester and give you grief for weeks after. When you live in these parts, you learn to share yourself with your neighbors. That is why it is said that tea is grown with sweat and blood.

In all this bounty, the thought that stayed with me was, 'What will I do when I retire? Or even before that, if I should need to leave planting for any reason?' This was because like any highly specialized career option, planting was only good for planting. Meaning that the direct skills are not transferable to other industries. To make matters worse, recruiters in other industries have no experience of planting and have no idea about the daily challenges that a planter faces. Recruiters of non-planting industries have a Tolly+Bollywood impression of the life of a planter. According to them, planters spend most of their time being waited upon hand and foot by an army of servants presided over by a butler and their main focus is a round of golf at 4.00 pm every afternoon followed by propping up the bar in the local plantation club. That is why there are very few success stories of planters making it big in other industries.

A planter, if he utilizes his time properly, is training to be a polymath. I don't know of any other career which provides this opportunity. Except that even most planters are not aware of what the career has the potential to provide. The challenges a planter faces, unremarked and unknown to outsiders, range from handling labor conflicts which can sometimes escalate to life threatening levels, negotiating settlements, building bridges, both real and metaphoric, surveying and laying roads, taking care of the welfare of workers and their families, running schools, creches, hospitals, temples and stores; and in my case building a tea factory. Dealing with government officials, contractors, labor union leaders, politicians, teachers, doctors, tractors, machinery, trucks and elephants who decide that walking on top of your aluminum water pipeline and making it crack, is such an entertaining activity. All this ends up making a highly competent and versatile personality but sadly the 'outside world' has no clue. So, planters plant until they can plant no more and then retire to two-bedroom apartments in a city and live out the rest of their days dreaming of days gone by. I was very sure that I was not going to be a part of that.

I loved every minute of my life as a planter. I became very good at what I did. I acquired a reputation for being effective especially in high tension situations with troublesome labor. This was thanks to my conditioning by fire in Guyana, which is another story. But that came in very handy in the Anamallais. But I knew that this couldn't last and that if I didn't prepare myself, I would have no alternatives to fall back on. The big question was, what could I do while remaining in planting, both because I loved the job and because I needed it. I had to train myself for another career while doing a full-time job in this one, with no money to pay for the training. Quite an interesting problem, if you ask me. It was then that I attended a training session in the Clarks Amer hotel in Jaipur. It was a two-week experiential learning session conducted by ISABS (Indian Society for Applied Behavioural Science) where you sat on the floor and learned to get in touch with your feelings, observe your own and others' behavior, give and receive feedback. Why sit on the floor? Well, we are Indian, you see; so, we sit on the floor, even when we never do that in 'real life'. That was an expression I learnt there and so deduct two weeks from my age as that was not 'real life'. However, what opened my eyes was the value of leadership development and how this could become a very satisfying career. The challenge for me was two-fold. There were (and are) no formal courses which one can take to qualify as a leadership trainer. And location wise, I was sitting in the hills while all the action in this line was happening in the cities. What I did and how I did it is another story. But for now, I want to talk about a very important lesson that I learnt; the real meaning of opportunity.

Commitment is the line you cross between wanting and doing. Unfortunately, most people never actually cross the line. They argue that they did not have the opportunity. This may be true in some cases, but in most it is commitment that they did not have; the opportunity was always there.

The reason why many people don't seem to get enough commitment to accomplish large goals is rooted in two causes:

1.	Lack of clarity about the benefits at the end.
2.	Impatience – giving up midway due to lack of immediate results

Clarity about the end

It is in the nature of extraordinary goals to inspire extraordinary effort. Nobody rises to low expectations; people rise to high expectations. It is essential that the final result is visualized clearly and is as real as possible to the person who sets out to accomplish it. The more desirable the final result, the more people will be willing to take the inevitable drudgery and the mundane, which is a major and essential part of all endeavors. It is the promise of great reward that drives the soul when the body has passed the boundaries of exhaustion. It is the expectation of that which is dearest to the heart that holds the hand when the night is dark and cold, and you are alone.

I became most aware of the power of the extraordinary goal when I was in Vietnam, fifteen feet underground crawling through the tunnels where the Vietnamese fought the Americans. I was doing the tourist routine in Cu-Chi where the tunnels are, wondering what it must have been to experience the real thing. The Vietnamese Tourism Authorities have widened one of the tunnels slightly and strung a couple of light bulbs so that it is not pitch dark. The tunnel is just about hundred meters long. You go down through a trap door at the bottom of which the tunnel begins. You have to lie flat on your belly and crawl. Does wonders for your clothes. Then at the end of the tunnel you come out into the pit at the bottom of the other trap door and climb out. And of course, you don't meet a snake coming the other way, nor are there bombs falling overhead. I was drenched in sweat to the extent that my shirt was soaking wet. There were two-hundred-and-fifty miles of these tunnels at three levels. They had hospitals, ammunition dumps, sleeping quarters, eating quarters, meeting rooms, and even burial rooms. They were cold and dark and damp. And overhead flew the American B52 bombers whose instructions were to drop all they had after every bombing sortie in this area. The Americans tried everything from flooding, gassing, chemicals, and napalm. Yet the Vietnamese fought back, often using discarded ammunition, booby traps made from empty Coke cans, nails, spring steel, fire ants, scorpions and snakes. Talk about invention and ingenuity. Talk about a very nasty way to die. Do that tour and then see the Vietnam War Museum in Ho Chi Minh City (Saigon) and you will learn the meaning of determination and resilience. Read about these in the books that are for sale there. Read also about the Tunnel Rats – American, Canadian, and New Zealand soldiers who volunteered to go into the tunnels and fight the Vietnamese, working alone. Makes you wonder what motivates such people. Irrespective of what one may think about the justification of the Vietnam War, one can only admire the courage of the soldier who chose to go into a tunnel, often with nothing more than a knife or a hand gun. The tunnels were built for the small, wiry Vietnamese, not for big Americans. So, it was the small, short ones from the American Army who volunteered. Amazing stories of some very brave people on both sides.

What kept the Vietnamese going? The same thing that kept Nelson Mandela and Ahmed Kathrada alive and mentally healthy for eighteen years on Robben Island. The same thing that drives the freedom fighters of today wherever they may be; the drive for freedom.

Freedom is a very powerful goal. A very basic and intense need of the human being. It is something for which a person will sacrifice anything. That is what those who seek to enslave forget; the fact that paradoxically, enslavement strengthens the desire to be free. The more you try to enslave, the more people want to be free. And in the end, the slave masters always lose. It is the thought of freedom that kept the Vietnamese fighters alive and striving for their goal for twenty years. Thousands of them died and never saw the goal fulfilled, but in the end, it was their sacrifice that ensured that the most powerful nations in the world had to retreat.

Giving up midway

Have you ever seen a traditional weighing scale in a shop in India selling food grains? There is an extremely important life lesson to be learnt from this. The next time you go to buy rice or some other grain, notice what the seller does.

First, he puts the weight measure in one pan. Say twenty kilos. Then he uses a scoop and starts to put rice into the other pan. As the pan fills, even when he has put nineteen kilos in it, what change do you see? Nothing.

There is no change in the situation. The pan with the weight remains firmly on the counter top and the pan with the rice remains in the air. However, the man does not stop putting the rice into the pan. He continues to do that until he sees a small movement in the pans as the pan with the rice starts to descend. Once that happens and the pans are almost level, the man changes his method of putting in the grain. Now instead of the scoop, he uses his hand. He takes a handful of rice and very gently he drops a few grains at a time into the pan. And then lo and behold, the pan with the rice descends to the counter top and the pan with the weight rises in the air.

When I saw this, I learnt two essential lessons in life, both equally true:

Lesson # 1:   Up to nineteen kilos, nothing will happen.

Lesson # 2:   At 20 kilos, the pan will tip.

Believing in the 'impossible'

Finally, if there is one thing that my life has taught me, it is the truth of the fact that nobody knows the best that they can do. This of course does not mean that you act with all passion and no planning. Passion is the key. Then comes the hard work of planning, scheduling, monitoring, measuring, taking feedback, course correction, and the final results. This is where the gap is created and enthusiasm fizzles out. However, if you plan well and make a good road map with milestones, then it helps to keep the passion alive. More importantly it helps to keep the passion kindled in the hearts of your followers.

Any great enterprise needs people. People who you can share your vision with, people who resonate to your tune, people who can hear the drumbeat to which you are marching. This is the biggest challenge that any leader faces. How do you make others dream your dream? Like most things in life, this also involves a paradox. On the one hand, as I have said earlier, the goal must be big enough to make it worth the effort. But a big goal is scary, and it can scare away a lot of people. On the other hand, if you water it down, then it will attract the wrong kind of people and fail to arouse the interest of those who can potentially share your dream. So, the goal must be big and exciting, even scary. Then it must be reduced into steps on a plan that will convince people that it can be accomplished. It is possible that you may end up with a plan that does not completely add up and leaves some room for a leap of faith but remember that if the gap looks like the Grand Canyon, it is unlikely that you will find any takers for your vision. There can be a gap, but the gap must be reasonably feasible. This is the beauty of a real stretch goal. It is big enough to excite and energize, yet not so big that it scares people away into not trying at all.

A good plan with graded steps plays the role of bringing the stars within reach. It also indicates that enough thought-share has happened in the genesis of the plan. Potential supporters look for this consciously or unconsciously. For example, when venture capitalists are listening to a business plan, more than looking at the numbers, they look to see if there is enough passion behind the idea, if enough due diligence has been done, and if enough alternatives have been generated and answered.

Generating alternatives is all about thinking outside the box in terms of what you do. Of using your creativity to approach problems from a different angle, which often opens doors that you did not imagine, existed. Taking advantage of opportunities is therefore more about commitment than about some unique, inspirational idea.

Corporate life - Choices

OUT OF SIGHT, out of mind is an old proverb that applies very much in corporate life. This refers both to being physically away from the corridors of power and those who walk those corridors as well as being in physical proximity but so silent as to become invisible. I recall a colleague who spent his entire career as an accountant in the same post, position and chair. When he was about to retire, I happened to visit his office, I noticed that the arms of his wooden chair and the edge of his desk had gentle grooves corresponding to where his arms had rested for thirty-five years. The grooves and their edges were also darker colored in mute testimony to the fact that the man had literally sweated at his desk. I hope his employers were appreciative of his loyalty. Most likely they didn't even notice. If they had, they would at least have got the man a new desk and chair.

I mention this because about five years into my career as a tea planter, I was promoted and transferred from the Anamallais to Assam. I was in two minds about accepting this position as on the one hand I would have had independent charge, but I would have been as far away from Chennai, our headquarters as is possible to be without going over the border into Nepal. I had advice from an unexpected source; the wife of my boss who had transferred me. My boss and his wife were both dear friends, but my boss was a typical career manager whose first concern was always what was good for the company, not necessarily for the person. His wife told me exactly that. She said, "Don't take this job. You will disappear from the radar and be forgotten. You will get labeled as an Assam planter which in a South Indian company with most of its operations in the south, is not an asset. Others will get the jobs down here and you will never return. You will do a good job there as you have always done which in this case will go against you as you will become indispensable there and will never be moved." I told her, "But (her husband and my boss) is advising me to go." She replied, "He is my husband and I know him better than anyone else. He is thinking of himself, not you. Your going to Assam will be good for him as he will have someone reliable there. But it will be oblivion for you." This is advice and a demonstration of integrity and genuine concern that I will remember lifelong. I declined the promotion.

In the corporate world it is important to be physically visible, not only through reports. Paradoxically if you are doing well and all your reports have nothing to make anyone concerned, you are not rewarded but forgotten. It is indeed the squeaky wheel that gets the grease, and this is nowhere truer than the corporate world. This was a trying period because suddenly I had no specific job. I had to leave my job as the Manager on Lower Sheikalmudi Estate because that job had already been assigned to another colleague. That left me literally homeless as there were no bungalows in the Anamallais where I could live. I was sent off to the Mango Range until the management could decide what to do with me. I was assigned a bungalow in a forest thicket, which was in a dilapidated condition. The location of the bungalow was lovely, and it was a joy to wake up to bird calls every morning. However, the house itself looked like it would collapse on our heads at any time. Of particular concern were the walls, which were so waterlogged that they had fungus growing on them in huge patches. My wife is an amazing homemaker and all her talents were put to test in this place. Out of this dilapidated house she created a lovely home which we enjoyed living in.

Since I had no regular job, I decided on doing two things:

For a long time, I had been talking about the need for systematic training of new managers. The current system in the plantations was that a new assistant would be put under a manager and what he learnt or didn't depended on the capability, interest, and energy of his manager and field or factory officers. If the assistant was lucky and got some people who were both knowledgeable and interested in teaching, then he learnt a great deal. If not, he remained guessing. This is a highly undesirable system, which is very time and energy intensive and does not give standard results. I had been saying for several years that there was a need for a standard text book on tea plantation management, which could be used to provide standardized training. Any additional inputs that the young man's manager and staff could give him would only add to this, but he would not be deficient in the basics.

During my stay in Mango Range, I decided to write this book and in 6 months, I produced a 200-page Manual of Tea Plantation Management. At the time of its publication there was no such book on the market and it was a source of great satisfaction for me. My company published it as an internal training book and though it was never a commercial publication, it did get fairly wide publicity and was used by many new managers. It has since gone out of print and to the best of my knowledge, it has not been reprinted. A big lesson for me was the power of the written word and its high credibility in making your customer base aware of what you have to offer. After that book there was no way that I could be ignored, not that I feared that. I had a lot of people who I had dealt with over the years rooting for me in the company.

The second thing I did was to spend a lot of time in Mango Range factory and hone my expertise in CTC manufacture of tea. I was very fortunate in that Mr. T.V. Verghese, who had retired as a General Manager in Tata Tea and was consulting with our company on manufacture, was a regular visitor and we became good friends. He shared his knowledge freely and I learnt a great deal. He was a practical teacher, which meant that I got to spend a lot of time on my back on the floor meshing CTC rollers with grease anywhere on my face and body that grease would stick. I learnt all aspects of manufacture hands-on, further reinforcing my belief that learning comes from doing – not from talking about doing. In Murugalli Estate, I'd had a lot of experience in Orthodox manufacture, and even though I had built Mayura Factory, the premier CTC factory in South India, I was moved as soon as the construction was over – thanks to a motorcycle accident. Consequently, my knowledge of CTC manufacture was weak. In Mango Range, as a student of Mr. T. V. Verghese and thanks to his willingness to teach, I rectified that deficiency. It was ironic that thereafter I went to Ambadi, which was a rubber plantation and never really used this knowledge, but it did come in use for writing a paper comparing Orthodox and CTC methods, which I presented at the UPASI Annual Conference in 1989.

Mango Range was an interlude in my career. I was marking time and waiting for some positive change to happen, and in the meanwhile I enjoyed myself. It has long been my philosophy to live one day at a time and to try to create as much happiness for myself and around me as possible. I have learnt that the two are the same. You can only be happy if those around you are happy. This is true whether you are an individual, an organization, or a country. Imagine what a wonderful world we would have if instead of competing, we collaborated and shared resources. We would all be wealthier, happier, and healthier. I have always held that the secret of happiness is to be thankful for and enjoy the small things in life. There are far many more of them than the big events. If we can enjoy the small things, then we can be happy all the time. The key to enjoyment is to appreciate them and be thankful for them. The key to contentment is not amassing material but being thankful for what one has. The happiest people are those who are content. Content people are those who are thankful. Material wealth has nothing to do with it.

One of the things that I was very appreciative of and thankful for, was the leisure that I had in Mango Range. I had no specific work except what I decided to do for myself. And I was still getting my salary. I decided to learn golf. I got a caddy from Ooty Club to come and stay with me in the estate for three weeks. His name was Frank Augustine (I used to call him Frankenstein) and he looked like a dried prawn. When he swung the club though, he always hit the ball with that sweet 'phut' that all golfers love to hear. And the ball would travel straight like a bullet down the freeway. Shows that technique and not strength of the arm is what works in golf. Also, in many other things in life. Whereas my club would come up with a good measure of earth and top the ball to boot. Frankenstein believed in hard work – meaning, making me work hard. He set up a practice net, produced a set of a hundred used golf balls and we were good to go. I would hit the ball into the net until I felt my arms would drop off. All the while, Frankenstein would sit on his haunches under the Champa tree that was to one side and watch me and make clucking noises. The effect of all this clucking and my swinging at the ball became clear when one day about midway in our training Frankenstein suggested that we should go and play a round at the club. So off we went on the three-hour drive to Ooty. After a cup of tea and a sandwich, I teed off and that is where all the practice paid off. Ooty Club has very narrow freeways bordered by spiky gorse. If you didn't hit your ball straight, you would send it into the gorse and then you may as well forget about it – or pay to get the ball back by leaving your blood on the gorse and acquiring gorse thorn furrows in your hide. As Frankenstein continued his mother hen act, I could see the distinct improvement in my style and capability.

Another one of my joys while living in Mango Range was the time I got to spend with Mr. Siasp Kothawala at his lovely guesthouse in Masinagudi called Bamboo Banks. Masinagudi is in the foothills of the Nilgiris at the edge of the Mudumalai-Bandipur National Park, so there is a lot of wildlife around. You see a lot of Chital, some Gaur, and some elephant, the latter being dangerous as they are too close to human habitation and often in conflict with people. Mudumalai is also supposed to be a tiger reserve though I have never seen a tiger in it. Perhaps it is another case of tiger reserves having been freed of tigers as has happened in many places in India. Anyway, my wife and I used to go to Bamboo Banks on some weekends. The gate of Bamboo Banks was an ingenious contraption. It was a pole, suspended horizontally across the road and had a plastic water container on one end. There was a sign asking you to tug on a rope if you wanted to open the gate. The rope was connected to an overhead tank so when you tugged it, water would flow into the plastic can on one end of the pole, which then went down and lifted the other end. All this happened while you were comfortably sitting in your car. The water would then drain out of a hole in the can and flow into an irrigation ditch and on into some fruit trees, closing the gate. Siasp was a tea planter and worked for the Bombay Burma Tea Company (BBTC). He then went into the tourism business and has done very well. We would spend lovely afternoons talking about the tea industry and the general state of the world and drinking tea. Siasp always had an angle to everything, which he would put across in a hilarious and entertaining way.

Siasp also had horses on his farm and having had tea I would take one of the horses and go riding in the sanctuary. This had its exciting moments and I recall two of the best. One day, late in the afternoon, I was riding out of the farm and into the dry fields that surrounded it before the track entered the bamboo thickets that bordered Mudumalai, when I saw a falcon hovering in the sky ahead of me. I pulled up to watch it and saw a dove break out of cover from a hedge and head for the safety of the forest flying very fast. The falcon folded his wings and stooped, coming down like an arrow out of the heavens. The dove had almost made it to the forest cover when the falcon hit it in middle of its back with a slap that I could hear where I was sitting on my horse. The dove must have died with the impact, but the falcon bore it to the ground and then holding it in its claws, looked up right and left, its pale-yellow eyes scanning the world to challenge any takers. What a magnificent sight that was. The image is engraved in my memory.

As I rode on, I took a path that went along the middle of a forest glade which had scattered clumps of bamboo. After a kilometer or two, the path passed between two very thick and large clumps of bamboo and dipped into a dry stream bed and went up the other bank. I used to like to gallop this stretch and my horse knew the routine. Strangely, on that day as we came near the bamboo clumps my horse shied and stopped and refused to go forward. This was odd behavior, but I have enough experience to know that in the forest your animal is your eyes and ears and you only ignore its signals at your own peril. I listened to the horse and turned around and then took a long and circuitous route to go around whatever it was that was bothering my horse. As we came around, I saw what was bothering him. It was a lone male elephant which was hiding behind the clump of bamboo. Now I have no idea what the elephant's intention was, but I was not taking any chances. My horse obviously didn't like the idea of passing close to the elephant and if we had continued on that track, we would have encountered that elephant where the path was the narrowest and where it was bordered and hedged in by the bamboo. In case of an attack, we would not have had any escape. Lone elephants are famous for such attacks. A rather terminal situation which we were happy to have avoided.

On one of those trips to Bamboo Banks, I saw an elephant by the roadside, a little way inside the forest. As this was quite close to the Forest Department's housing and elephant camp, I thought that it was a tame elephant and decided to take a picture. I had a small box camera at the time in which you were the telephoto – if you wanted greater magnification, you had to go closer to the object. I got out of the car and walked almost to the side of the elephant and took a photo. Suddenly I heard someone yelling at me, his voice high pitched in panic. I looked up and there was a forest guard, some good two-hundred meters away, waving frantically and yelling at me to get back into the car. Since it is not an offence to get out of your car on the main road in Mudumalai, I was irritated at this man's insistence but since I already had my picture, I returned to the car. As we drove on and came up to him, the man waved us to a stop and still in an angry voice asked me in Tamil, 'What do you think you are doing? If you want to die, go do it somewhere else.'

I said to him, 'Hey! Relax. What is all this about dying? I was only taking a picture of one of your elephants. Who said I want to die?'

The man said, 'Our elephants? That was a lone wild tusker that you were standing next to. I have no idea why he let you get that close or why he did nothing. Your lucky day. That is a wild elephant and a lone one at that. Don't do these stupid things.' And he went on for a while in the same vein. I was so shocked that I listened in silence. And of course, how can you get angry with someone who is only interested in preserving your life? But I still have the picture, which is very impressive.

Life Lessons from Tea

I STARTED WORKING in India in the Anamallai Hills, part of the Western Ghats as they tapered down all the way into the tip of the subcontinent. Before that I had worked for five years in bauxite mining in Guyana, South America and lived on the bank of Rio Berbice, in the middle of the Amazonian rain forest. But that is another story.

The area that contained the tea plantations was part of the Indira Gandhi National Park. The park is home to an amazing variety of wildlife which thanks to the difficult terrain, plethora of leeches, and shortage of motorable roads is still safe from the depredations of 'brave' hunters buzzing around in their Jeeps and shooting animals blinded and frozen in their searchlight beams. In the Anamallais if you want to hunt (it is illegal to shoot anything in the National Park, but there are those who are not bothered about what is legal and what is not) you must be prepared to walk in the forest, up and down some very steep hills, be bitten by leeches and have a very good chance at becoming history at the feet of an elephant.

However, if you are not interested in hunting and killing animals, you have all the same pleasures and thrills with the animal healthy and alive at the end of it. I want to see and photograph animals, not kill them. I have hunted enough in my youth and lost interest in killing things as my connection with nature strengthened. I was looking for an opportunity to just spend time in the environment that I loved. My job as an Assistant Manager in Sheikalmudi Estate, my first posting with a princely salary of ₹850 per month, gave me all that I could have wished for.

Sheikalmudi borders the Parambikulam forest. This extends from the shore of the Parambikulam Reservoir (created by damming the Parambikulam River) up the steep mountainside all the way to the top. Sheikalmudi is the crown on that mountain's head, manicured tea planted after cutting the rain forest, more than a century ago by British colonial planters. Where the tea ends, starts the rain forest of the Western Ghats. Anamallais is the second rainiest place on the planet. In the early part of the century it used to get more than three-hundred centimeters of rain annually and consequently it rained almost six months of the year. Even when I joined in 1983, we frequently saw spells of more than a week at a stretch, when it rained continuously day and night without any easing of the volume of water. I was horrified the first time I saw this. I was used to rain in Hyderabad, where we get about thirty centimeters annually. And to the rain in Guyana, where because of the Trade Winds which brought the rain, it rained on most days in the evenings for a little while and then cleared up.

Now here was rain and more rain and more rain. Yet in all this rain, we went to work at 6.00 am every morning. Heavy canvas raincoat, waterproof jungle hat, shorts, stockings and wellingtons. We rode our motorcycles down treacherous hill pathways, slippery in the rain and covered with fog as sometimes a cloud decided to rest on its journey across the sky. It was very cold because we were between 3500 to 4000 feet high and so in the first ten minutes, you lost all feeling in your legs, below your knees.

Walls of the bungalow would have mildew growing on them in damp patches. Small leaks would develop in the roof and their yield would be received in sundry pots and pans placed under them. This would create its own music. Little frogs would emerge from every crevice and would hop all around the house. In the night, they would find some resting place and add their voices to the night chorus of frogs and insects in the garden, that would rise and fall like an animal breathing. But sometimes the rain would be so heavy that all you could hear was the rain on the galvanized iron sheet roof. This sound would drown out every other sound. Within the first week of the beginning of the monsoon, all telephone lines would be down. Power supply would become extremely erratic. And more often than not, landslides would block roads. So being cut off from everyone for several days was a common phenomenon. When there came the occasional storm – every year we used to have at least two or three – all these problems would get magnified.

Candle light dinners with a roaring fire in the fireplace were the fringe benefit of this weather. That and in my case, a lot of chess by the fire. The year I got married, 1985, there was a storm in which twelve-hundred trees fell on my estate alone, taking down with them all power and telephone lines. There were two major landslides and we were cut off from the world for a total of fifteen days. It rained almost continuously for this period and my poor wife had a wet introduction to the new life ahead of her. But typical for us both, we enjoyed this time, playing chess by the fireside. She started by not knowing chess at all and I taught her the game. By the end of our enforced seclusion she was beating me. Now take it as her learning ability or the quality of my game, but being rained-in has its benefits.

I have always looked for challenges. Anything that comes easily does not excite me. My learning, that it is the extraordinary goal that inspires extraordinary effort is very personal to me. In the plantation industry I was constantly focused on setting new records. And over the years I was able to do this in all aspects of tea and rubber planting. I set the record in yield per hectare, in work tasks in various cultivation activities, and in the price of the manufactured product. I reclaimed swamp land and planted cardamom and set up bee hives and produced cardamom flavored honey. I reclaimed illegally cultivated land bordering our tea and planted tea in it adding over 50 hectares of land to the estate. I planted vanilla under rubber and successfully pollinated and harvested the vanilla bean; to my knowledge the first time this had been done in South India. When I say, 'I', I mean my team. I had one of the best in the world, each of them close friends who worked with me with total devotion and dedication and who I was very proud to call my own. I trained several of them, when they came to me as probationers and while not all were equally happy during the training, as I am a hard task master, every one of them was thankful for what they received and have remained lifelong friends.

1983-86 were boom years for tea in South India. Anything that was produced would sell. The biggest buyers were the Russians who bought on the rupee trade agreements between the governments of both countries. Anything that could be manufactured in South India was bought by the Russians. Sadly,

58

quality went out the window. Some people, including myself, were able to see the writing on the wall and tried to get manufacturers to focus on quality and to get out of the commodity market and instead create brand. That, however, meant investing in brand building and hard work in maintaining quality standards. Since people were making money, nobody was interested in listening to anything that meant more work or investment. Eventually, the inevitable happened. Russia collapsed and so did their buying trend and it almost took the South Indian tea industry down with it. Some companies shut down. Others were more fortunate. But the whole industry faced some very hard times.

Interestingly, success seems to breed fear of failure. This is a paradox, since success should really build confidence. It does that too, but what seems to happen over the years is that we become progressively more afraid of losing what we have created and our ability to take risks decreases. This to me explains why entrepreneurs who have built large organizations are so afraid to allow others to take the same kind of risks that they took when they were alone and creating the company. Somehow, as they succeed, people who build organizations seem to forget the real lessons of their experience:

- That it was speed of reaction and the ability to take risks that gave them the competitive advantage.
- That it was the willingness to put themselves on the line, which built their credibility.
- That it was staying in touch with customers that helped them anticipate trends.

This fear of taking risk seems to extend even more to their own children, a phenomenon that we see in many family owned companies where the old, often senile, patriarch rules supreme and holds the strings of power. That is also why such organizations finally break-up, usually with a lot of rancor, as the rebellion against authority comes to a head and the son has no alternative but to break away. This fear of failure has many respectable names: Consolidation of gains, Stability, Creating Permanence and so on.

What is forgotten is that life is about change and positive change is growth. That growth is not looking inwards with a satisfied glow at what exists, but always to seek what might be. And that all growth is essentially characterized by a lack of stability, living with impermanence and spending what you have, to fuel what you aspire to create. This is forgotten, not by chance or accident. It is forgotten deliberately, albeit sometimes unconsciously. And it is done to deal with the fear of failure if one continues to take risk.

So, what is the alternative?

In my view, the alternative is to practice change even when there is no need for it.

Some organizations create think-tanks whose job is to conceptualize hypothetical threat situations and suggest solutions. One can use this or any other method, but it is a very good idea to spend some time and energy in anticipating the future and preparing for it. I personally make it a point to do this kind of reflective observation every so often. The important thing is to make this an ongoing process, no matter how you do it. Anticipating change is the first step to creating game changers that will put you in the driving seat. That is the only guarantee of permanence in a world where permanence is against nature. Any other route in my view only guarantees stagnation of ideas, sanctification of monumental stupidity, and calcification of the mind.

The single biggest and most critical requirement of success in my view is the desire to be the best. No matter what you may do – if you want to succeed, you need to be passionate about what you do and want to be the best at it. This is something that I have been aware of in myself all my life. I always wanted to be the best at whatever I did. Read the most, get the best results at school, train my dog so that it would win in tracking and show championships, school my horse so that he would win in dressage competitions every time, climb the biggest mountain I could find, do what nobody had done before, go where nobody had gone before me. Always trying to excel in whatever I put my hand to. I never saw any thrill in simply doing more of the same. I always wanted to do something new. And that's a very cool way to live.

It is not that I succeeded on every occasion. But I made a serious effort every time. And when I failed, I used the other technique that I had learnt early in life; to analyze failure, face the brutal reality, and acknowledge ownership. No justification of mistakes. No blaming others. Take the responsibility for my own actions. See what went wrong and why. See what I need to do to ensure that this particular mistake never happens again. The pin and hole principle in engineering; fool proofing the system so that it becomes impossible to make a mistake. Not leaving the issue to individual discretion but creating a system to ensure that the correct procedure is followed every time. These are two principles that I have always tried to follow in my life: try to be the best and own up to mistakes.

A third principle that I have always tried to follow is to actively seek feedback. And then to listen to it without defensiveness. No justification or argument with the person giving the feedback, always remembering that my intention is inside my heart. What we intended to convey is less important than what we did convey. What the other person sees is the action, not the intention. And if the action did not convey the intention, then the action failed and must change, because for us all, perception is reality.

Being passionate about what you do is absolutely essential for anyone who wants to be the best in their work. For me, this has never been a matter of choice but something that I have always held as inevitable. If I do something, then it must be the best that I can possibly do. Nothing less. I discovered that if I am in a profession or job where I can't really find it in myself to be passionate about it, then I need to change the job. And I did. Happiness is not doing less. It is to do the most that we can do. To maximize contribution. And that can only come through loving what you do. I am deliberately using a term which is not often used in a work context, love. People who don't love their work are stressed. People who love their work automatically get a sense of meaning from it and believe it is worthwhile. The more they do, the happier they are. They get stressed not with work, but with not having enough of it.

Just to close the point, a working person spends roughly thirty to thirty-five years doing what we call work. If we take a lifespan of seventy years and subtract the years spent in childhood and education, work life is almost seventy percent of a person's lifespan. To spend this doing something that does not give fulfillment, satisfaction and a sense of achievement, but is something that is routine, boring and even unpleasant, is a very stupid way to live your life. Unfortunately, that is how many people do lead their lives. In dead end jobs with no value addition to themselves or to the organizations they work for. That is why work produces stress.

Life in the Anamallais passed like a dream. Berty Suares was the Assistant Manager on the neighboring estate, Malakiparai. And Sandy (Sundeep Singh) was on Uralikal. Both dear friends. They would come over to my place and we would spend Sunday picnicking on the bank of the Aliyar River where on a bend in the river that passed through our cardamom plantation, I had built a natural swimming pool. I deepened the stream bed and deposited the sand from there on the near bank, thereby creating a very neat 'beach.' Sitting on this beach under the deep shade of the trees after a swim in the pool was a heavenly experience. Add to it, eating cardamom flavored honey straight from the comb, taken from the many hives that I had set up in the cardamom fields for pollination. The flavor comes from the pollen of the flowers which the bees take to make the honey. Depending on where you set up your hives or where the bees go to find pollen, honey can have as many flavors as there are flowers. While we lazed about at noon, our lunch would be brought down to us and we would all eat together. The joys of being a planter in the days when we had people who knew how to enjoy that life.

If you walked down the river for a couple of kilometers you would come to the Parambikulam Dam backwaters into which this river flowed. I had built another pool there at the bottom of a waterfall, thanks to a stream that flowed through Murugalli Estate. We used to keep a boat in the dam to go fishing on the lake. There was a thickly wooded island in the lake about half a kilometer from the shore on which one could go and spend the whole day, swimming and lazing in the shade; a very welcome occupation, free from all stress. The only sounds that you would hear would be the wailing call of the Rufus Backed Hawk Eagle and the Fishing Eagle. In the evenings, Jungle Fowl called the hour. If you stayed beyond sunset, the only danger was that you could encounter bison (Gaur) as you walked home. That encounter was not something to look forward to as I discovered one day. Mercifully, I was walking softly and the wind was in my face, so the Gaur was as startled as I was. He snorted, spun on his heel, and vanished, crashing through the undergrowth. I was very fortunate.

The more time I spent with myself, the clearer it became that it is important to be 'friends' with yourself. The more you are self-aware and comfortable internally, the more you can enjoy the world outside. When you are not aware of what is happening to you inside or are unhappy with decisions you have taken, or with your own internal processes, the unhappier you are likely to be with your surroundings. The normal tendency is to blame the outer world, but if one looks within, it is possible to find the solution. One rider however, that you will find only if you seek and only if you have the courage to recognize what you see. That is where sometimes the matter remains unresolved. Not because there is no solution. But because we are unwilling to accept the solution or to implement it.

Time for another dip, then climb into the hammock and gently swing in the breeze that comes blowing over the water. Those were the days……………………

My Extended Family

THE TEA PLANTATIONS of the Sub-continent are a unique environment, be that in South India, Assam or Sri Lanka because they represent a completely artificial man-made community. The areas where tea is grown were, until a hundred years ago, pristine rain forest. Then came the British, having discovered wild tea in Assam as well as with stolen tea seedlings from China, which broke the tea monopoly of that country. Workers were transported from the plains of Tamilnadu for South Indian and Sri Lankan (Ceylon) plantations and from Orissa and Bengal for the Assam gardens. In South India most if not almost all of them were Dalits. They were housed in colonies according to their native areas. They built temples and either one of them officiated as the priest, having learned the rituals in Eklavya tradition (unofficially from some kind priest who would teach him) or they hired a poor Brahmin, who because he was paid by them, didn't prevent them from entering the temple. This was not the case (and to this day it is not the case) in their own homelands, where Dalits, though officially classified as Hindu, are not permitted inside Hindu temples. This resulted in an egalitarian tradition which continues to this day, where everyone participates in all festivals and religious functions. The estate manager especially, irrespective of his religion, is expected to officiate at all religious functions of all religions and is specifically invited as the Chief Guest. Generally, this merely means putting in an appearance and flagging off a temple procession or lighting a lamp to signify the beginning of a ceremony or some other symbolic gesture. But it is nevertheless important and taken very seriously.

There is a book called Red Tea, by Paul Harris Daniel, which is a novel but is based on fact. The author took sworn affidavits from those whose stories he told. This book was published by Higginbotham's in 1969 and was later made into the Tamil film 'Paradesi'. The book gives a good account of what life in the early plantations was like and what the real price of tea is, not in money but in lives and blood of animals and men. Not to speak of the tremendous damage to the rain forests of Northeast and South India and Sri Lanka (Ceylon in those days). But those were the days before there was any awareness about these things and after all we were a colony to be exploited for the benefit of the British Empire and so we were; thoroughly.

When I joined planting in 1983, this was all history but there were still old workers who had seen a lot of what I have written above. One of them was Kullan, who was in his 70's when I met him in 1983. We would sit on my veranda in the night and he would tell me stories about the 'old days' (Palaya Gaalam). That is the benefit of learning the language (Tamil, which I didn't know a word of until I joined planting) and of having a good relationship with your workers. It was in the course of one of those sessions that he told me in a very matter of fact tone that the bungalow in which I lived (where we were sitting right then) was the estate hospital in those days and in the monsoon when there was an epidemic of cholera, many bodies were simply thrown into the ravine that was a little way behind the bungalow. "That is why their ghosts are still wandering here, Dorai", he said to me. I must say that none of them ever bothered me, though Kullan was not the only one who mentioned ghosts in that bungalow.

The Muslim workers in Murugalli Estate where I was posted decided to dismantle the temporary shed that they used as a masjid and build a small, but permanent concrete structure in its place. They had collected some money and the company also gave them a small grant. But when they did the math in the end, they discovered that they had no money for the centering sheets to cast the concrete roof, nor did they have money for the labor to cast the slab. They came to me for advice to resolve this issue. I spoke to Mr. Dakshinamurthy, the Mayura Factory, Site Engineer, and he readily agreed to loan them the centering sheets free of cost. He also loaned them the concrete mixer. All that remained was the labor. I suggested to them that we do a working Sunday and get all the Muslim men to help with the labor and the Muslim women to make some food.

 "Why do you need to pay for labor to build a masjid when we are all here?" I asked them. They all agreed enthusiastically. So, the following Sunday that is what we did. What fun we had!!

The Muslim workers in Murugalli were all from the Mallapuram district of Kerala. The women made some wonderful Malabari Biryani and we started early in the morning after a large mug of highly sweetened Malabari tea. We set up a human chain from the mixer to the top; I was on the top. The men started a chant in Malayalam as they passed up the concrete containers and we started pouring the concrete. This is a job that needs to be done without stopping, so as the day advanced and we became tired, the work became progressively more difficult. But the spirit of the work, the fact that we were building a masjid, and the promise of the Malabari Biryani, which was making its presence felt as its aroma floated on the air as it cooked, kept us going. By late afternoon the final load was cast, and we came down. Then after washing up, we sat down to a meal that was more delicious than I remembered eating ever before. Was it the food? Was it the hunger? Was it the fact that we were eating it after a day well spent? I don't know. All I know is that it was wonderful to eat.

There is a sad ending to this part of my story. Dakshinamurty suddenly died in a very bizarre accident. He was at home one weekend and was having his head oiled. The barber who did the oil massage for him twisted his head to crack his spine. This is a very common practice in India and is done all the time without any adverse result. However, in Dakshinamurty's case the man accidentally snapped his spinal cord. He was instantly paralyzed from the neck down and two days later he passed away. Sadly, he could not see the completion of Mayura Factory, the project that he had started. D.R.S. Chary stayed with me till the project was completed and then returned to Chennai where he lived. A couple of years later, I heard that he also passed away. I mourn the passing of these good people with whom I shared some wonderful times.

When Mayura was finally built and was to be inaugurated, Mr. AMM Arunachalam sent priests to do a puja – Ganapathy Homam (Havan), which was to start at 2:00 am the next morning and would go on for several hours. Once the puja was complete, we got ready for the formal inauguration to which the entire

Board of Directors was invited including the Chairman Mr. AMM Arunachalam. This was followed by a lunch at the Group Manager, Mr. AVG Menon's bungalow in Sheikalmudi. The building of Mayura Factory was a truly historic occurrence because tea factories are not built every day. Most in the Anamallais were over eighty years old at the time Mayura was built and commissioned (1985). On top of that it was the largest and most modern factory in India with computer-controlled systems and all kinds of bells and whistles. Since I was the man on the spot, so to speak, I had to be in many places at once and managed to do it. Everything went off well. Lunch finished late and we returned home close to 5:00pm. I had been awake and working for 48 hours straight with perhaps a short nap on my feet. But the day had not ended yet for me. We, my newly wedded wife and I, had a formal dinner to attend in Mudis.

Among the customs of plantation life was that of 'calling on' the seniors of the district. When you came in new or got married and your wife came to the estates, you called on the seniors of the district to introduce yourself and her. You telephoned or sent a letter saying that you would like to call on them and asked when would be convenient. These were formal social meetings and you were treated with great dignity and grace. This 'calling on' was usually for tea unless it was somebody you knew already, in which case you would be invited to dinner.

We had just got married (March 1985) and I returned with my wife, post haste to the estate because Mayura Factory opening was due. Two days after our marriage we boarded the train for Coimbatore from where we drove up the Aliyar Ghat of forty hairpin bends. My wife was violently sick all the way up the

Ghat. Being prone to motion sickness, the Ghat road was not doing her any good at all. I was very concerned because this Ghat road was a given if we lived in the Anamallais and with my wife being so sick on it, it didn't seem to portend well for us. The prospect of a repeat performance every time we traveled was definitely not something to look forward to. But as it happened after a couple of trips my wife got over her motion sickness altogether. Maybe the Ghat road shocked it out of her system.

As was the custom of the plantations when anyone got married and returned with his wife, there was a round of parties to meet the couple. So also, in our case and since I was the Secretary of the Anamallai Club, I had more than my fair share of friends and so we had a party to go to every night. The parties were formal suit and tie affairs and the hostess would go to great lengths to cook special dishes in honor of the guests and at the end the couple would be given a gift. In a place where social relationships were very important, these parties were not simply for entertainment. They were rites of passage and thresholds of entry from bachelorhood to marriage, which gave you a higher level of status and respect. They also had a 'snob value' associated with who invited you and who didn't. I didn't bother with that at all, but then again, I was invited by everyone, so it didn't matter. The parties were also a good way to introduce the new bride to a way of life that was foreign to her and helped her to make contacts with senior ladies and others more experienced in this lifestyle, which could be challenging for someone born and brought up in the city. Most people who go to tea gardens for a holiday in good weather don't realize the difficulty of that environment for those who must live there all year round.

The estate workers also welcomed the Assistant Manager when he returned with his wife. In my case, the Candoora workers were the first. As our car rounded the bend off the Sholayar Dam and came towards 'Black Bridge,' we were stopped and requested to alight. We both came out of the car, glad for the chance to stretch our legs. The road was lined with girls who sang a welcome song and showered us with flower petals as we walked through this guard of honor. We were taken to a small pavilion which I realized had been made by tying the best sarees of the women to the poles and decorated with lots of flowers. Tea garden workers can be the most loving people in the world and if you are good to them, they appreciate it and reciprocate. I saw many examples of that in my decade long career. We were garlanded and sat at a table on the two grandest chairs that they could find. Then we were served tea with biscuits and sweets. It was then that a depressed fly decided to end its meaningless life in my wife's tea cup. But my wife being the perfect lady that she is, merely fished out the fly and drank the tea without batting an eyelid. An amazing performance which saved us from a lot of embarrassment. Those poor workers had taken so much trouble to welcome us that it would have been very ungraceful to complain, even about the suicide of a fly.

Then speeches were made, and the women danced and sang another song in our honor in which we were mentioned repeatedly in sometimes a humorous way and sometimes with great respect. The amazing thing was that this song was made up then and there and they sang about various habits of mine, including singing while I rode my motorcycle. People observed you and remembered and mentioned what you did. All the more reason to ensure that whatever it was, remained good and honorable. At the end of this song and dance there were some speeches by the local union leaders and one supervisor and then I was asked to speak. It was permitted for the manager to speak in English and the speech would be translated. But I had learnt Tamil for occasions such as these and spoke it well, much to everyone's delight. When I had finished and thanked them for all their trouble and expressed our gratitude for the honor that we had been granted, they gave my wife a gold ring as their gift as a mark of their love and honor for me. I was floored. These were poor people who had collected money for this, something which was not expected of them at all. What could I say? As I mentioned earlier, Managers and workers in the plantations form bonds that are more like family than anything else.

To return to the daily dinner parties in our honor, these daily night outings were so frequent that my wife could recognize a road only in the dark. The parties, enjoyable though they were and were a good way to meet friends who lived too far to visit frequently, could be very taxing as they tended to go on very late. I was expected to put in an appearance at the morning muster on the estate at 6:00 am no matter when we returned. The night of Mayura Factory inauguration (the day that started at 2:00 am), we had been invited to dinner at the home of our dear friends, Prema and Ricky Muthanna in Mudis. Ricky was the General Manager of BBTC and we were honored to be invited to their home. As it happened, there was no time even for a short snooze in the afternoon thanks to the inauguration and to top it all, my car was once again in hospital. I didn't fancy the idea of going all the way to Mudis (about thirty km on serpentine estate roads, decorated with potholes) on my motorcycle. I asked AVG

Menon to borrow his new car, an Ambassador, for the evening and he graciously agreed.

We set off at about 7:00 pm as the dinner was for 8:00 pm. I was exhausted as I had been awake for 48 hours, but we set off, my wife and I, on this long drive. We arrived at Prema and Ricky's house to a very warm welcome. My wife and Prema became friends instantly and have remained friends all these years. Ricky and Prema's home was a delight, very tastefully decorated and one of the iconic bungalows in the Anamallais. It was the only bungalow to my knowledge which had a central courtyard with a veranda all around it and so it had a garden inside and outside. Prema had called a lot of people in our honor and the house was full of our friends and some others who I knew by name but was meeting for the first time.

All plantation parties (except in my house) started with drinks, which the men consumed in large quantities while the women sipped soft drinks and discussed matters of great import. As I was not one for the spiritual experience, I would take my orange juice or fresh lime soda and chat with whoever was still on mother earth. But as many left for higher altitudes in proportion to the spirit inside them, I would usually take myself off into a corner and contemplate the world. That day I was so sleepy and tired that my eyes were self-shutting unable to withstand the weight of my eyelids, while the party was in full swing. I was clearly out of it. Prema saw me in that state and said to us, 'Yawar looks like he is going to drop. Let me give you dinner so that you can eat and leave. I have no idea when these men will eat, and you look like you won't last too long.' I agreed wholeheartedly, and we ate, said our farewells quietly and left.

Even up to that point I had my faculties still intact. You had to be alert when driving in the Anamallais, both because of the road conditions as well as the possibility of coming upon a herd of elephants or gaur around a bend. That night was mercifully elephant free and we reached Lower Sheikalmudi Estate without incident. As I took the final turn on the road leading up to our bungalow (the 'Tennis Court Bungalow'), I relaxed and that was my undoing. The next thing I knew, there was a crash and the car came to an abrupt halt. I was shocked back into awareness and realized that I had driven off the road. The left front wheel of the car was hanging off the side of the road in midair with the front fender resting against a tea bush, which was the reason we didn't go all the way down into the ravine. The chassis was resting on the road bed. My wife and I were shocked. It was 2:00 am and there we were.

I realized that this was not a good situation because the car didn't belong to me. It was Mr. Menon's car and a new one to boot. It was therefore my responsibility to get out of this situation. It didn't even occur to me that I could leave the car where it was until morning and then get assistance to take it out of its predicament. I had crashed it and it was up to me to get it out. And I had to do it right away; it was not even a matter to think about. As it was, the car was directly below a stairway that led up to our house. I got my wife to walk up to the house so that she would be safely home. Then I went in search of a tractor to pull the car out. I knew that the leaf transport tractors – Massey Ferguson – used to be parked near Mayura Factory, about two kilometers from where I was. Our roads had no street lights and it was a dark night. The tea fields were home to wild boar and other friendly species, not to mention several species of snakes, but none of them was my boss while AVG Menon was. So, I hiked off in search of a tractor. On the way I called my good friend, mechanic Thangavelu, because there was no way that I could pull the car out alone. He and his ever-present smile came out of his house as if he had been waiting for me. Both of us got to where the tractors were parked and selected the one we wanted.

None of the tractors had self-starters and used to be parked on an incline so that you could roll down and start the engine. And they had no lights; I never understood why. Working in starlight, I got into the driver's seat, rolled down, and started the tractor. Now we needed a tow rope. Thangavelu recalled that the telephone company people had been working on a line passing through one of our fields and had left a coil of telephone wire there. So off we went, with Thangavelu standing on a plank behind me, holding the seat as I drove the tractor. We picked up the coil of wire and drove back to where the car was; hooked up the wire to the chassis at the back and pulled the car back on the road. When I examined the damage, I saw that the tea bush had taken the shock and except for a small side indicator light, nothing was broken. That was a big relief to put it mildly. Thangavelu and I, then took the tractor back to its parking spot and I drove home at 3:30 am. I still recall the first thing that AVG asked me when I told him that we'd had an accident in his new car. He said, "I hope you both are alright?" I told him that we were fine but that his new car had been inaugurated with a broken indicator light. He was amused and laughed it off and said, "That can be fixed. I am happy that nothing happened to you both."

That is why we used to call him A Very Good Menon (AVG Menon).

Tea Factory, Black magic and Demons

ONE OF THE first things that strikes you as you enter any 'Tea District' is the tea factory. These in many if not most cases are over a century old, build entirely of wood on a structure of steel girders. The machinery, especially in the Orthodox factories is fit for a museum. For the uninitiated, 'Orthodox' refers to the type of manufacture and not the religious inclinations of the manager. This was the case when I entered planting in 1983. Then in 1985 our company, Parry Agro, decided to build a spanking new CTC (another way of manufacturing tea) in the Anamallais. I was closely associated with the project from the word 'Go.' The factory was built on Lower Sheikalmudi Estate and AVG Menon, my first manager was made responsible for the project, since he was the Group Manager for the Sheikalmudi Group. He appointed me as his assistant for the day to day supervision of the construction and so I became the defacto Site Manager of the project. At this time, I was the Assistant Manager in Murugalli Estate with responsibility for Murugalli Factory (Factory Assistant). I now had two jobs, reported to two managers and no additional pay. I was delighted, and it didn't even occur to me to ask for more money for doing almost double the work that anyone else was doing. Not because I am allergic to money but because I was going to get a chance to build something that others had only done a century ago; build a tea factory.

I lived in a bungalow that was midway between Murugalli Factory and the site of the proposed Mayura factory and was the proud possessor (company issue) of a Royal Enfield 350 cc motorcycle. This ran on a mixture of petrol and faith aided by gravity when coasting downhill after its engine periodically decided to give up the ghost. I would then roll down the road to its end and hand over the bike to its resurrector, Thangavelu, our mechanic who had no formal education in automobile engineering but could make anything with wheels run, when all others had given up on it. It was (and is) a fascinating fact about our tea gardens, factories that for literally over a century, they are run by people like Thangavelu who learnt their art as apprentices with some other mechanic and run machinery that would be a major challenge for highly qualified engineers. These people have no diagnostic tools, no meters, just a spanner and a pair of pliers; but with that they moved mountains. This is an unsung lot who work from generation to generation and disappear quietly into the environment, none the wiser or even grateful that thanks to them, they (the unwise and ungrateful) got their daily cuppa.

Thangavelu looked like he had lube oil in his veins. His clothes looked like leather, thanks to the amount of oil they had absorbed. He had three teeth in his top jaw and a few more in the bottom, all visible because he never stopped smiling from ear to ear, come rain or sunshine. He never walked. He trotted. His heart was made of gold and he was my brother. He still is, and now retired, I hope he has a long and happy life. Apart from his genius with motorcycles, he repaired tractors, cars, factory machinery and worked a lathe machine. I wanted a pruning knife, a wicked blade 18 inches long and curved at the end, sharp enough to shave the hair on your arm (that is how we used to test it). Thangavelu started with a broken piece of truck spring blade and created a knife nestled in a handle made of Sambar horn (they shed annually), bound with brass hoops. It was a work of art and I had it for many years, until the Deputy Forest Officer coveted it and expropriated it in exchange for releasing ten of my workers who got arrested for killing a barking deer. But that is another story.

I mentioned Thangavelu because I mentioned my Royal Enfield motorcycle, my sole means of transport. And that, because one day it died. Truly forever. That left me in the situation where I was in-charge of two projects, Murugalli Factory and the Mayura construction project and no transport. I asked my Manager who was my immediate superior and who had not been happy at all at my appointment with additional responsibility for Mayura, if he could let me have another bike. He said to me, 'Who told you to accept the additional responsibility? Now ask whoever appointed you.' That meant that I was to ask AVG Menon who had asked for me. I refused to do that as I had no intention of getting in the middle of company politics. In any case, I was very pleased with the appointment and didn't want to go to AVG with this kind of stuff. So, I used to walk every day twice, to both factories, clocking in about 15-16 kilometers all told. That continued until one day I was hoofing it when a car drove up from behind me and I heard a cheery, 'Hello! Yawar!' It was Mr. Rawlley, the Visiting Agent (an old British period title that was still used in those days even after the Agency system no longer existed), on his inspection tour of our group of estates. 'Why on earth are you walking?' he asked.

I told him the story and that evening, much to my manager's acidity and flatulence, I got a new bike.

Mayura was unique for many reasons. For one thing, it would have a capacity to process one-hundred-thousand kilograms of green leaf per day. At a time when the average production was two-thousand-five-hundred kilograms made-tea per hectare, this was a huge figure, one that nobody thought could ever be reached. It was the vision of Mr. K. Ahmedullah and Mr. N. K. Rawlley, who were the General Manager and Visiting Agent respectively. They proposed the theory that creating capacity would stimulate production as it would put pressure on the estates to supply the factory. Initially, nobody believed them except the Murugappa family; Mr. Alagappan and Mr. AMM Arunachalam in particular. But that was enough as they were the ones who were funding the project. Once the factory was completed, Ahmed's and Nickoo's vision was proved right. The production of the estates went up from two-thousand-five-hundred to four-thousand kilograms per hectare. Needless to say, this did not happen by magic. A lot of people put in a lot of effort, but there is no doubt that it was the presence of Mayura that pushed us all to excel. Once again this proved to me the value of vision.

Since the Anamallais is hilly, locating a huge factory was no easy task. It involved leveling the land first, to create the construction site. The main building was on columns, but we still needed a level site to locate all the rest of the buildings and bays. We had two bulldozers brought up from Coimbatore to do the cutting and filling of soil on the hillside to get enough level land to start building. I went down to the site on the first day that the work started. The bulldozer operators were already on their machines with the engines running. I called the leader of the team to give him instructions. He switched off the engine and came to me. I showed him from which part of the hillside I wanted the soil to be cut and where I wanted it to be moved and dumped so that eventually we would get a flat surface. He listened in silence, then handed me the key and said, "Why don't you show me how to do it?"

I was taken aback by this obvious insubordination so early in the morning. But I took the key from him, climbed up on the track of the dozer and into the seat. I started the engine, engaged gear, and started cutting the soil. I worked for about half an hour. Then I parked the machine, switched off the engine, got off the machine, and handed the key back to the driver and walked away, all in silence. I had a hard time keeping a straight face at the look of shock on the driver's face for having called his bluff. The long and short of this was that I never had a problem with that driver again for the duration of the land clearing stage. When the work was done, and the drivers were going back, he came to me and said, "I apologize for challenging you on the first day, but tell me where did you learn to drive a bulldozer?" I told him, "In future, before you challenge anyone, find out what they know."

My knowledge of bulldozers and machinery was acquired in Guyana in the mines, when I was doing a Job Evaluation exercise in the company and had to evaluate the difficulty of each job. Knowing how to do the job yourself is obviously a big advantage and not one that most non-technical people have. I had very good relations with the bulldozer, truck (50 ton CAT dump trucks) and dragline crane operators and they gladly taught me how to drive them. For them I was a curiosity, a young Indian boy in his early 20's willing to learn from grizzled West Indian African experts whose hands were like steel encased in sandpaper. That I was their superior in rank meant nothing. That I was willing to learn and not throw my weight around meant everything in my favor. I was welcomed. We joked, shared our meals and I spent many happy hours in the cabin of a truck or bulldozer deep in the Amazonian rain forest or in the great mine pit.

My learning in this incident of the bulldozer at Mayura fatory, many years later, was the fact that to build credibility it is important to be able to lead from the front. You don't have to do people's jobs for them. It is not even desirable to do this. But you do need to demonstrate that you know what they do and can do it if necessary. It is when subordinates get the impression that you know nothing about what they do, that it makes them nervous and lose motivation. The good ones feel a little lost. The crooks take you for a ride.

Mayura Factory's construction was a time of learning for me. The site engineer was a wonderful elderly gentleman called Mr. D.R.S. Chary, who stayed with me in my bungalow throughout the project. He was a very well read and learned man, many years my senior but with a great sense of humor. We hit it off from the first day and became great friends. Chary taught me a great deal about constructing large buildings. I found this a fascinating time and used every opportunity I could, to add to my knowledge. On the factory site, the contractor's site engineer was another wonderful man called Mr.

Dakshinamurthy. He also became a good friend and was helpful in many ways.

Chary and I lived in the bungalow behind the tennis court. We could see the construction site from our veranda. Since Chary was a Brahmin, out of consideration for him, I had instructed my cook and butler Bastian, not to cook any meat while he was staying with us. No meat was cooked for over six months in our kitchen. I would go to some of my other friends like Berty Suares and Taher for my meat fix.

The bungalow had a somewhat shady history in that it was supposed to have been the estate hospital in the remote past during an epidemic and many people had died in it. It also had the dubious distinction of having a resident demon. There was a small shrine at one end of the garden, which I was told was a shrine to Karpuswamy (literally means: Black God), who the people described as a very powerful and evil entity that needed to be placated with an annual animal sacrifice. The sacrifice itself was not done in the Bungalow garden because it was done at a larger temple, but every morning one of the tea plucker women would put some flowers at the shrine. Chary, like most highly educated Hindus, did not believe in any of this, given more to keeping to the social norms than any real religious belief in the mythology.

Some weeks after Chary and I moved into the bungalow, some rumors started to circulate in the estate to say that my bungalow was haunted and that people had seen Karpuswamy near the bungalow at night. I saw nothing and was not perturbed by the rumors. I don't believe in ghosts and don't believe that anything can harm or benefit anyone except the Creator Himself. I slept well. Chary told me one day when he was leaving after the completion of Mayura Factory that he never seemed to sleep well in this bungalow. But I was not sure how much of that was because of some unconscious effect of the rumors and how much of it was plain indigestion or some such thing. He was over sixty years old at the time, after all.

I had recently bought a used Ambassador car. It had the dubious distinction of having belonged to the son of Marri Chenna Reddy a former Chief Minister of Andhra Pradesh. Among its other attributes was the fact that it was graced with a carburetor that was cracked down the middle and was held together with a wire. Now hold on – before you go making sly remarks about Ambassadors, ask yourself, 'which other car would still run in this condition?' And run it did. However, it did need long hours in the workshop. In the plantations the workshop came to you, as did most other things. One night, Velayudhan, the mechanic, was working on the car in my garage behind the house. He worked late into the night and promised to return the next day to complete the job. The next morning there was no sign of him and when I sent someone to look for him, the man returned and said that Velayudhan was in hospital.

I was very surprised and concerned as the man had been working in my house the previous evening and had been well and healthy. What could have happened to him for him to be hospitalized? He was a cheerful and willing worker and I had a very good relationship with him, so I was genuinely concerned for him. I went to the hospital and first asked the doctor what the matter was with Velayudhan. The doctor told me that he had been brought to the hospital late the previous night in a hysterical state, his heartbeat racing and in a semi-conscious state. He was so bad that the doctor had been afraid the man would have a heart attack or a stroke. All this seemed to have been brought about by intense fear. He had to be given a heavy dose of sedative to put him to sleep. In short, the man had been extremely frightened by someone or something.

I went to see him and he told me the story, which I present to you without comment.

He said to me, "Dorai, I had finished my work for the day on your car and decided to take the short cut through the tea field down the hillside instead of the main road. It was a full moon night and the footpath was clearly visible in the moonlight. As I started down the path, I suddenly heard a heavy snort behind me, like a cow sometimes makes as it is grazing. I looked back over my shoulder and saw a huge man with flaming red eyes and huge teeth. I turned and ran and then I fell down and fainted." Some people who were going past on the main road below heard the sound of his running and then saw him fall. They picked him up and took him to the hospital. There was some suspicion that perhaps he'd hit the bottle, but the doctor denied that and said that he did not show any sign of having been inebriated. He was just very badly terrified and completely hysterical with fear.

I lived in that bungalow for two years and went in and out at all hours, but never saw a thing. That is what led to the rumor that Karpuswamy was the guard on the bungalow and guarded me.

In the plantations such rumors add to your mystique and reputation. In any case, I could do nothing to refute it.

A year later, another incident added some more grist to the mill.

There was a supervisor who was very corrupt, so I dismissed him. He was naturally very upset and angry with me and threatened me with many things. He did not say any of this to me directly of course, but various rumors started floating that he would do black magic against me. Black magic is quite prevalent in India and in the plantations and many people claimed either to do it or had been its victims. When these stories got to me, I said, "If anyone does anything against me, it will turn against him. I worship Allahﷻ and nothing can happen to me without His will. I ask Him to protect me." That put a stop to all the talk that came to me.

Then one day, I was walking in the field with my Field Officer Mr. O. T. Varghese, a wonderful elderly man who taught me a lot about tea planting. Suddenly a tea plucker woman came running to us, wailing all the while and fell at my feet. She was wailing, "Only you can save me. Have mercy on my husband……" and so on. I was taken aback to say the least. After a while, Mr. Varghese and I managed to get some sense out of her. Mr. Varghese told me that she was the wife of the dismissed supervisor. She told us that her husband had gone to a black magic expert in their village and asked him to put a spell on me to kill me. However, the spell backfired on him and now he was dying and was in hospital, where they had brought him the previous evening. She begged me to go with her and see her husband.

I agreed, though I thought to myself that this was a jolly good thing and served him right for his efforts. After all, his wife had not tried to stop him from his nefarious activity and if he had succeeded, his wife would have been sitting pretty with him and not running to my aid. Anyway, Mr. Varghese and I reached the hospital and I asked the doctor about the patient.

He said to me that there was nothing wrong with him except that he was in a state of very high excitement and terror and had not slept for more than 72 hours. His heart was racing and the doctor was fearful that if he continued in this way for a few more hours it was entirely likely that he would have a heart attack. I entered the room after getting this information. As soon as I entered, the man literally fell off the bed and put his head on my feet. Weeping, he cried, "Dorai, please forgive me. I tried to do something bad to you, but it has come to me. I have children Dorai and they will become orphans if I die. Please forgive me Dorai and take this thing away from me." It was the strangest experience that I have ever had in my life. I told him to get up and pulled him up by his arm and put him back on the bed. Then I asked for some water and recited Sura Al Fatiha (the first chapter in the Qur'an) and the Al Muwaddathian, the last two chapters and blew on the water and told him to drink it. I told his wife to give him what was left of the water later in the evening. Then I left. The doctor told me later that shortly thereafter the man slept and the next morning he was discharged.

Never a dull moment in the estates.

What did you see?

KABINI RIVER RESORT on the bank of the Kabini Reservior, bordering Nagarhole Tiger Reserve. I am in the Gol Ghar (which is actually rectangular) at tea and snack time after the afternoon safari.

"What did you see?" asked an American who had come to Kabini for the first time.

"Nothing. Totally dry. Five safaris and we saw nothing," said an extremely bossy Indian woman whose rude behavior was on display wherever she went with the saving grace that nobody was exempt from it. One must be grateful when people with bad manners display them equally for everyone.

Ajeeb! I say to myself. Then I check to see if the people talking were blind or blindfolded. But no. They weren't. Bright eyes and each had a camera and lens worth at least 3 – 4 laks each. One a Nikon and the other a Sony. But we shall not hold that against them. What was more, this conversation or different versions of it, were happening all around me. So, it wasn't only this one woman who saw nothing.

How could this be? How can people go for a three-hour drive in one of the most beautiful forests in India and say that they saw nothing? Unless of course one were to ask, "What does seeing mean?"

Well, what did I see?

I saw a silent life and death struggle between a strangler fig and its saprophytic host, a nameless giant of the forest, whose fate was sealed when the first tender filament of the fig started its climb upwards towards the sun. After that it would only be a matter of time, measured in decades perhaps, but the ending, inevitable. The fig strangles the host. As I saw this struggle without motion, I thought how closely it resembles what is happening in our national politics. Politicians of all hues have taken hold of the nation like strangler figs and are busy throttling its life out. There is one exception to this however in our case. Unlike the forest giant, we the people of India, are not helpless. Unless we choose to be. We are not helpless unless we choose to vote for the one who gives us Rs. 200 instead of voting for the one who is most likely to serve our best interests. Rs. 200 doesn't even buy a chicken. Is this what we have priced our futures and the futures of our generations yet unborn, at? Less than the price of a chicken?

I saw Chital (Axis deer) or Spotted deer in their hundreds. Chital is one of the most beautiful of the deer species. In Nagerhole, they abound. Grass and shrubs are aplenty. The terrain suits them very well. There are predators; Wild dogs (Dhole), leopards (black and regular) and tigers but the Chital simply outbreed them all, so they thrive. Predators also ensure that all the weak die early and only the strong are left to breed so predation helps and promotes survival of prey species. I saw their fawns ranging from some which must have been literally days old to older ones. Chital fawns simply must be the most beautiful creatures on earth. All Chital have liquid black eyes with eyelashes that will give every Bollywood actress a complex. Their coats, golden brown with white spots showing shadowy in the morning mist are a sight to behold.

Then their behavior; the way the dominant alpha males strut. The stags with a full rack of horns, which they shed every year to grow a new pair; clothed first in skin called 'velvet' which they then rub off on trees until it is at first hanging in rags and then is totally cast away to show the shiny bone beneath. It is rutting season and you can hear the territorial braying call of the alpha males, challenging all takers. The stags eat very little during this time, being focused almost entirely on protecting their harem of hinds from other roving males, ready to give battle at the slightest provocation. When there is none they sometimes take out their testosterone on innocent bushes, bashing then to smithereens with their impressive horns.

But if you are a Chital, no matter how impressive, you are at the bottom of the food chain. Everyone eats you and you eat grass. So, if you want to survive and live to tell tales of your life to your grandchildren you need to be extremely alert. Chital learn this lesson early in life. Those that don't, never grow old. The result is that Chital will sound their typical alarm that sounds like a very high-pitched bark, at practically every suspicious movement. I have seen Chital calling when they see a Sloth bear, Dhole, Wild boar, eddies of wind rustling the bushes and simply because they imagined that they saw a tiger or leopard. But you can hardly blame them for this because they are No.1 on the menu of any predator on a keto diet. One of them calls while striking the earth with one forefoot with every call. The rest, run. Chital learn two CTS (Critical to Survival) lessons in life which are good lessons for us to learn also.

Lesson No. 1: Complacency is death.

Lesson No. 2: It is better to run twice than to be caught once.

A much more reliable alarm giver is the Grey Langur. These have a symbiotic relationship with Chital. Langur feed in tree tops and drop more than they eat, of leaves and fruit which the Chital eat off the ground. And all bands of Langur have a sentinel, who doesn't feed but sits on the highest branch of the tallest tree in the area and scans the forest for threats. When he sees anything suspicious, he calls the alarm and the Chital take off. Since this sentinel is watching from a vantage point, he is much more accurate in his risk assessment. When his shift is over, another of the tribe takes over and he goes to feed. It is amazing to see how this entire system works to the advantage of two different species who are united in threat. How much can we learn, I muse, about being united despite our differences because we face the same threats in our societies. Threats of moral degradation, drug abuse, unemployment, domestic violence, rape, murder, crime of different kinds; all of which don't differentiate between us because criminals view all victims equally. Makes the forest with its lurking leopards and tigers seem positively safe.

Langur are playful in the extreme. Most amusing are the young. They fight, chase each other up and down trees, making some leaps which almost amount to flight. I saw one young chap simply hanging from a vine and swinging back and forth. Just like a child on a swing. He was simply having fun. Another one climbed up behind his older sibling and used his tail for a swing. That didn't last too long because the owner of the tail had a different opinion about this liberty. Some older individuals simply sit on a branch with their hind legs stretched out before them. Occasionally those lower in the pecking order come up behind them and start grooming them. I saw one Langur sitting on one branch and leaning out holding another with his hands while resting his chin on his hands, fast asleep. His instinct ensures that he doesn't let go of the other branch even in his sleep. Our driver stopped the jeep under a tree, but noticed some Langur sitting directly above and very wisely and hurriedly moved us out from beneath them. I could almost hear one of them look down at us and say to the other, 'Are you thinking what I am thinking?' I didn't fancy being the recipient of their donations.

Nagarhole seems to have the highest population of Hoopoes and Flame-backed Woodpeckers that I have ever seen anywhere. Both are beautiful birds with the FBW males shining like jewels in the forest. They fly in their characteristic wavy flight and land on a tree trunk (unlike all other birds that land on branches) and immediately switch to the back of the trunk. Very infuriating because my camera can't see through the tree. The females are not as colorful as the males, as is the case in most species of birds but have the same flight pattern and irritating habit of hiding from you.

Trying to match the FBW is the Indian Roller. A brilliant blue bird whose brilliant lilac breast and fluorescent blue wing colors are spectacular in flight. What is best about the Indian Roller is his desire to be photographed. He is totally unfazed by the jeep or the chattering monkeys in it. He perches on a solitary branch of whichever short tree or bush that happens to be present and watches intently for his prey; worms, insects and whatever is small enough to appeal to his palate. Then he flies down, picks it up and flies back up to the same perch to eat it. This is an absolute boon for the photographer who can literally set his camera and wait to get the in-flight photos which are the best for this bird.

Another extremely photogenic bird is the Green Bee Eater and its various cousins. They are best seen in the early morning and sometimes in the late evening. They perch on any raised object, a dry branch, a rock or even a blade of tough high grass and watch for flying insects. As soon as they spot one, they swoop up, pluck it out of the air and return to their perch to eat it. Once again, this predictability of returning to the same perch and the fact that they are not spooked and liable to fly away at the slightest movement, makes them such favorites of photographers. Their brilliant green plumage, with some blue in some of the sub-species, their feathers which closeup look very fine hair, black beaks and shiny black eyes are a study in art. Birds in general afford one a look into their lives and behavior much more closely and readily than mammals and so are wonderful to photograph. Naturally, given their size (small birds) and that they fly about means that you need a camera and lens that can get you close to them. But if you have that, then there is endless joy in photographing birds.

As I was trying to find a better perch for myself in the jeep that had (believe it or not, eleven adults in it) the driver whispered to me and I looked up to where he was pointing and loed and beheld a pair of Imperial Pigeons. They were in a fig tree, engrossed in gorging themselves on the fruit. While I took pictures of them, there was a shadow and the pigeons exploded out of the tree and headed for the Lantana bushes. I looked up to see a Brown Serpent Eagle. Pigeons are not his normal diet, but I am sure it wouldn't object to a change of menu; something the pigeons understood very well. The eagle settled on the fig tree and so there was no chance of the pigeons returning, but I noticed a Monarch butterfly alight on a blade of tall grass. One single butterfly on a single blade of grass in just the right light. As I was clicking away, I saw a flash of yellow and there were a dozen Clouded Yellow (I think!!) butterflies on a damp patch in the road. Butterflies of all kinds settle on patches of moisture in the road and make wonderful objects of photographs with their brilliant colors, set off against the brown or black background of the road.

The driver moved along as our companions were getting bored with not seeing anything. We drove around a corner and came to a pack of Dhole (Indian Wild dogs), resting in the grass under some trees. The Dhole is a rich brown in color all over with a pointed face and a black tail. It is barkless and whistles. The dominant female and alpha male were sleeping. A couple of uncles were also resting, but one of them was sitting up, alert and watchful. In the jungle you have two choices; be alert or be eaten. There were four puppies who were being the pesky nuisance that all young are when adults are resting. Whistling and nuzzling and trying to crawl under their elders, failing which climbing all over them. What was amazing was the patience of the elders, who couldn't have been enjoying this 'affection' but showed no irritation. The sentinel suddenly tensed but didn't sound an alarm. I looked in the direction that he was pointing to and saw the most enormous Gaur bull that I have ever seen. Huge and black with his signature white socks, walking slowly and majestically, fearing nobody and nothing. He was followed by three cows, one of which was a subadult and so much more skittish. But the bull was a sight to behold.

Just then a peacock screamed. What else can you call that sound? It is a communication call, 'See what I am doing!' What was he doing? Dancing to try to please a bevy of totally disinterested peahens. But he was spectacular to say the least.

Still not having seen anything, the driver decided to go and investigate why two other jeeps that had passed us, hadn't returned. We drove to a place where the road takes a steep dip between two low hillocks and there in the depression, we finally saw that after which we couldn't say, 'I saw nothing.' A tigress sleeping. Or more accurately, trying in to sleep. No sentinels here. Just a cat trying to get some sleep in a patch of sunlight while batting flies and mosquitoes which had other ideas. No sentinels because when you are the apex predator, you fear nobody and everyone else fears you. Our camera shutters sounded like machinegun fire as we took amazing action photos of a sleeping cat. Every time she flicked her tail, the cameras would go trrrrrrrrrrrr. Every time she rolled over they would go trrrrrrrrrrrrrrr. We watched her in action for over an hour, hunched up with our eyes glued to the viewfinders, our backs screaming in agony but who cares? A tiger is a tiger.

We returned with the light started failing and we had to get out before the designated time. "Did you see anything?" they asked.

"Yes," we replied. "We saw a tiger."

Nothing else, only a tiger. So, did we see anything or didn't we?

What do you say?

Jhalana Leopard Conservatory

Jaipur's secret paradise

THE BLUE BULL had been killed by hyenas. The Striped Hyena pack, led by the matriarch had lived in this forest for generations beyond number. Their ancestors lived off the kills of tigers, until the last of those great hunters fell to the guns of men. Men, forever on their quest to kill, burn and destroy and call it conquest. They hyenas didn't know all this of course. What they did realize was that one day, the roar of the tiger was not heard any longer. That brought about a great change in lifestyle for them. They turned from scavengers to hunters. Actually, that is a bit of a false blame. Hyenas are formidable hunters in their own right but when the pickings are easy, they make no bones about taking advantage. In this case, the old Blue Bull cow, actually India's largest antelope, called Blue Bull for no fault of its own, was sick and dying. She was sitting under an Acacia Juliflora (Prosopis juliflora) tree. Acacia Juliflora is an invasive weed from Mexico and the Caribbean that is found all over Africa, Asia and Australia today. Its major strength is that it has very deep roots, the deepest of any plant and so, is drought resistant and remains green in the summer. The major disadvantage is that it doesn't allow anything to grow under it. Its fruit is a bean which is very nutritious and so its seeds are spread far and wide by herbivores which eat the Acacia beans with great relish. When you have large stands of this plant, you will find the ground free from undergrowth and grass. A serious

The old cow was half asleep and unable to keep up with her herd, sat down to rest. She didn't even see the Hyena matriarch come up behind her and when she felt the bite on the back of her neck, her spine was already severed, and she couldn't move. The Hyenas ate their fill in the course of which they broke up the carcass into two just above the hindquarters. As the sun rose, the Hyenas moved off into the hills as they are almost completely nocturnal in habit. The carcass remained where it was, attracting others, smaller but no less hungry. The Jackals came first and dived head first into the abdominal cavity for the delicacy of the intestine. Not much was left but they ate what they could find. There are no vultures in this area or nothing would have been left for the leopard pair which came a little later.

Ancient instinct drove the leopard to first secure the kill from other predators and scavengers. The big male carried the front half of the carcass into the first fork, about 10 feet up, in an Acacia Juliflora tree and wedged the head into the fork to leave the neck and ribcage hanging down. The fact that this carcass probably weighed more than his own body weight means little to a cat which is, pound for pound, the strongest in the cat kingdom. There is no other feline which is stronger than a leopard which is why leopards regularly kill prey which outweighs them enormously. The Indian Leopard (Panthera pardus fusca) is smaller than its African cousin (Panthera pardus pardus) but not lacking in either strength or courage and tackles prey much larger than itself. In Jhalana though a full grown Blue

Bull is perhaps too big to be in any danger, leopards take subadults and calves when they can. Other prey they depend on are peafowl of which there is a large number. The Forest Department has attempted to introduce Cheetal (Axis Deer or Spotted deer) in Jhalana but with limited success. Another species which should be introduced is Wild Boar. Prey species are critical to the wellbeing of predators and most importantly, a means of avoiding wildlife-human conflict. When prey species are scarce in the sanctuary predators go into surrounding habitation in search of food and take domestic animals and sometimes humans, which has only one ending for the animal. Death. A very good example of excellent conservation is Yala National Park in Sri Lanka where thanks to a profusion of prey species, leopards stay in the park and human animal conflict is avoided. The Sri Lankan leopard is a different subspecies from its Indian and African cousins, (Panthera pardus kotiya) and has evolved to become a very large animal with habits of an apex predator which it is, in Sri Lanka which has no tigers.

The only contenders to the leopard's cache in Jhalana are Roufus treepies. Wikipedia says: The **Rufous treepie** (*Dendrocitta vagabunda*) is native to the Indian Subcontinent and adjoining parts of Southeast Asia. It is a member of the crow family, Corvidae. It is long tailed and has loud musical calls making it very conspicuous. It is found commonly in open scrub, agricultural areas, forests as well as urban gardens. Like other corvids it is very adaptable, omnivorous and opportunistic in feeding. I advise you to believe Wikipedia. As for opportunistic feeding, well, the first on the Blue Bull carcass in the tree, were the Treepies, picking off pieces of flesh from the ribs. They are so bold that they don't even care about the leopard when he and his sister come to feed from the carcass that they secured for themselves. They still pick pieces off the opposite side. The Hyena matriarch and her pack can only look upwards and salivate because the carcass is beyond their reach.

The amazing thing is that all this is not happening in some lost wilderness but in the heart of one of India's most beautiful and famous cities, known for art, craft, historical monuments and mouth watering cuisine, Jaipur. The great secret of Jaipur is Jhalana Leopard Conservatory. It is called Jhalana Leopard Safari; safari being a much-misused name for anything to do with wildlife as 'trekking' is used for walking one kilometer on a regular road, when you decide that you are going 'camping'. I think calling it Conservatory is more appropriate and will keep our attention focused on what we need to do to ensure that this remains viable and protected for wildlife to live and people to enjoy. Jhalana is 17.5 or 21 or 24 square kilometers in area, depending on who you ask. Typical hills of the Aravalli Range with quartz rock, dry deciduous forest and ravines where the run-off from monsoon rains digs ever deeper as it scores the land and carries away the soil. On the lower slopes running into flatlands, grass should grow and would, if it were not for the Acacia Juliflora which abounds here and doesn't allow anything to grow under it.

However, Jhalana has a very valuable resource; local people who are deeply interested in preserving the sanctuary and protecting its inhabitants. I had the privilege of having one of them, who I like to call their 'chief', be my companion and guide when I visited Jhalana earlier this week. He is Mr. Dhirendr

Godha, publisher of a Hindi daily newspaper and a great wildlife enthusiast and photographer. It was my good fortune that he agreed to take me on two drives in the morning and evening with spectacular results. I say that people like him are the most valuable resource because ultimately forests and wildlife depend on the support of the local population for their survival and protection. The general failure of wildlife conservation thanks to poaching and habitat destruction in India and the success in Africa show very clearly the importance of the support of local people for the wellbeing of animals and forests. In Jhalana this exists in the efforts of people like Mr. Godha who have dedicated their lives to this piece of paradise in the middle of a city.

My visit was arranged by my host, Mr. Rajesh Sharma, the publisher of Rashtradoot, who requested his friend, Mr. Sunayan Sharma, the former Director of Sariska and the man responsible for the successful reintroduction of the tiger into Sariska National Park, to facilitate my visit. To my great delight, Mr. Sunayan Sharma accompanied me himself and introduced his friend Mr. Godha, who arranged everything and came with us. The trip was an education for me in the flora and fauna of the region and the peculiar challenges to wildlife conservation in this region. Much of what I have written here is the result of the conversation I had with Mr. Sunayan Sharma who is a treasure of knowledge about the Aravalli Hills and its habitat. Having successfully reintroduced tigers into Sariska National Park from which they had been eliminated by poachers and widespread habitat degradation, his extremely practical knowledge about what works and what doesn't is a resource without parallel.

I am not merely praising these gentlemen here. I am saying all this in support of my earlier article on the challenges of wildlife conservation in India where I suggested involving young people from schools and colleges. This would need two things; easy access to forests and people with knowledge who are willing to share their knowledge. In Jaipur (Jhalana) both are present. A beautiful forest within half an hour's drive from the city. And people like Mr. Sunayan Sharma and Mr. Dhirendr Godha. I would strongly recommend that the Government recognizes such people and invites them to form a National Forest Core (like the NCC) which can educate young people about conservation. It is important to give young people a taste of the forest and its inhabitants, plants, animals and birds, so that they learn to love them. Give them memories that will last them their lifetimes. When that happens, they will stand up to defend what they love. Our forests today are the victims of apathy arising out of ignorance. A program like the National Forest Core can address and correct that.

To return to Jhalana, we saw a young female leopard eating from the kill on the tree, clinging to the trunk like a lizard. Leopards here are used to traffic and tourists and if you don't make too much noise they continue to do whatever they are doing, undisturbed. A great boon for photographers. After a little while she leapt to the ground and leisurely strolled away and entered a thick bush nearby. We knew that she would stay there until we had well and truly departed and so we left her in peace and proceeded homewards. The light was failing as dusk approached. As we took a turn in the road, we saw her brother, a young male, sitting just inside the tree line. He was totally relaxed and continued to sit there and even groom himself as we watched. As we had to leave the park and it was very close to the time the gates would be closed, we headed back. But just as we came to a watering point, a cement saucer made by the Forest Department and filled by tanker, we saw the mother of the two cubs, drinking. She appeared to be heavily pregnant, a very good sign. The water was green with algae which in itself is not such a problem but was also probably contaminated with urine which could lead to sickness for those drinking it.

This brings me to the close of this article with three recommendations about what I believe needs to be done in Jhalana urgently.

Remove the Acacia Juliflora immediately. This requires uprooting as it is a resilient plant and if cut, will simply grow back. Until this is done nothing will grow under it. This scarcity of fodder is lethal for herbivores and therefore for predators. The Forest Department has planted other species under the Acacia but these will never flourish or even grow as long as the Acacia is alive. The Acacia must go.

Plant grass after uprooting the Acacia. What can be done is to fence small areas, say about a quarter of an acre, and remove the Acacias in that area, plant other species and infill with grass. The fencing can be removed once the trees have come up well and are impervious to damage by herbivores. I saw that the trees planted by the Forest Department under the Acacia are individually fenced. But in the summer, it is a safe bet to say that the Neelgai and Sambar will get to them in their search for fodder, not matter how they are fenced. This won't happen if a large area is fenced, perhaps with solar powered electric fencing and the trees will have a chance of surviving.

Waterholes must be earthen floored. There are some excellent ones made recently with earthen floors lined with lime. Cement 'waterholes', which are really cement pans must be broken up. Herbivores, especially Sambar, walk into the water to drink and they urinate as they drink. Cattle do this also, especially buffaloes. In an earthen floored waterhole, this gets absorbed and the water remains relatively uncontaminated. In a cement waterhole, everything remains and it becomes highly toxic.

Finally, as I mentioned earlier, I believe Jhalana is a gift to Jaipur and an excellent environment to introduce young people to the wild. Combined with knowledgeable people like those I have mentioned and many others who live in the city, Jaipur can launch the National Forest Core. I don't know of any other city which has wilderness with so many different species of herbivores, carnivores and birds in easily accessible terrain. It is easily possible to have weekend camps and familiarization programs where young people are introduced to nature and wildlife and taught how to enjoy both safely and without creating any interference.

I firmly believe that the key to wildlife and forest conservation is the wholehearted support of local people. That can't happen when they don't know the forest, don't know how to conduct themselves respectfully and safely in it and so live in fear of forests and wildlife instead of loving and enjoying them. It is only when the young generation learns to appreciate nature that they will do what needs to be done to protect and preserve it.

What's my crime?

THE KILLING SHOT is just behind the shoulder. Aim for the spot behind the elbow and your bullet will tear through skin and muscle, enter the rib cage and pulverize the heart. If it gets deflected by a rib it will still go through the lungs and graze the heart enough to cause massive bleeding. But it is not a disabling shot. It will kill but after a while, when the thoracic cavity is filled with blood and the animal starts exhaling it, spraying trees and grass with its lifeblood as it runs, pain and fear crazed, trying to escape. Not knowing that it is already dead on its feet. All you need to do is to wait. Eventually, in agony that I can't even begin to describe and terror that only the one who feels it can know, the matriarch falls.

She was the repository of wisdom for her family. Wisdom learnt from her own mother and her mother before that, as long as elephants walked on the land. Wisdom which she taught to her progeny, especially her daughters. Wisdom which told her where to dig for water in the drought, which not only ensured the survival of her family but from which all other animals and birds benefited. Wisdom which reminded her of the best paths over mountains. Paths that men later converted to roads, so well 'surveyed' they were and suitable to movement of heavy traffic. Wisdom which told her where the best fodder was, the most succulent grass, new leaves on the Mopani and soil with salt and minerals which elephants need to complete their diet. She was the matriarch. They followed her, obeyed her, respected and loved her. Sometimes in their wandering they would come across elephant bones. The skeleton of another, long gone. She would stand by them in silence and they with her, handling the bones, gathering those scattered. Sometimes, covering them with leaves. She and they knew that one of theirs had died and they mourned their dead. The intelligence of the elephant and their close family ties are their burden.

But today, she had been mortally wounded and had fallen and lay dying. The herd, her children and family are also mortally wounded like her, also fall, one by one. The only ones' left are the calves. Nurslings, whose tusks have not grown yet. The tiny ones who are still nursing, dependent on their mother's milk. All their aunts, cousins, older siblings, are dying and have died in one manic morning of blood and death. The calves cry out; literally weep. Crying for their mothers and weeping with terror and grief because for the first time in their short life, she doesn't answer. The calf never knew this to happen before. His mother was always there.

He talked to her, threw tantrums, got smacked on his behind, walked under her belly if the sun got too hot, just reached up and drank his fill of milk if was hungry and simply lay down to sleep if he got tired while she stood over him to shade him, while he slept. If he strayed away from her, one of his aunts, cousins, grandmothers, someone was always at hand to answer, with a rumble, a honk or a comforting trunk on his head. But not today. Today he wails in vain. He cries out, screams in despair, but nobody answers him. His mother is lying there but doesn't respond. There is an overwhelming smell of blood and guts and dung. He is dazed and can't understand anything. All he knows is that his mother is lying down and no matter how much he cries and butts and nudges her, she refuses to get to her feet. He needs her, he is terrified, he calls to her, but for the first time, she is silent.

The hours pass, because elephants don't die easily. Then come the executioners. He smells the hated man-smell, as they come. Not with guns now, as they know there is no danger. They come with machetes and chainsaws. They come to his mother's body. He tries to protect her but they just push him aside. One of them slams his head with the butt of a rifle. The blow dazes him but he is still standing and watching as they hack away his mother's face. Where machetes find it tough going, the men use chainsaws. They rip out her tusks. Then they go to his other family members who are lying where they fell. Other men load the tusks onto a truck they came in. Two hours or so later, they are gone. All that is left is the smell of blood and the smell of man. And there is silence. It is then, that he hears something he recognizes. Not with any pleasure but with a strange fear that he had never felt when he heard it many times earlier. The laughing of Hyenas. He had not felt any fear as his mother and the herd was always there to protect him. But today?

For predators on the plains, elephants are almost impossible to kill. There is no throat to throttle, no neck to break. The only way that an elephant can be killed is by tearing off enough flesh to inflict wounds, grievous enough to create massive loss of blood, so that the animal falls. Then it can be eaten alive. It takes many hours of unspeakable agony for the elephant and normally can't be done to an adult. But a baby is another matter. Normally, no lion, leopard or hyena can even dream of getting close to a baby elephant. The herd is always there to protect the individual. But when ivory hunters have evened the odds in their favor, lions and hyenas are most thankful.

So, while one waits in dread, the other comes in anticipation.

I hope those who still insist on buying ivory ornaments, really like what they wear. They are the real killers. It is their fingers which are on the triggers of poacher's guns. Because poachers work for them. If there are no buyers, there will be no poachers. The real price of your trinkets is in blood, tears and unimaginable agony of innocents. Enjoy them!!

Future of wildlife conservation in India

ONE OF OUR big challenges in wildlife conservation is to stop poaching and habitat degradation which leads to animal human conflict which always has only one ending, destruction of the animal. The backbone of the conservation team in a Reserve Forest or a National Park is the Forest Guard. This individual lives inside the forest, many in the Core Areas in highly substandard conditions, is paid a pittance and is expected to be self-motivated enough to walk miles of boundary tracks to ensure that no illegal activity is happening. He is unarmed, except with a stick and walks as he has no vehicle. In many places where he is required to go there are no roads for him to use any vehicle, even if he had one. He lives away from his family who he sees perhaps once a week.

I am given to understand that the average age of the Forest Guard is 50 years and that young people are unwilling to take this job because of its hardship and deprivation. All these forests are starved of funds, thanks to our bureaucracy and many a time, even sanctioned funds are not released by State Governments. Be that as it may and no matter how unglamorous the job of the Forest Guard is, it is the most critical link in the chain that protects our wildlife and forests. It is critical that State Governments take note of the plight of these people and enhance their salaries and living conditions and do what it takes to ensure that they can do their jobs comfortably and effectively.

I firmly believe that the key to wildlife and forest conservation is the wholehearted support of local people. That can't happen when they don't know the forest, don't know how to conduct themselves respectfully and safely in it and so live in fear of forests and wildlife instead of loving and enjoying them. That is also why we see the completely despicable and deplorable behavior of people when they do go to spend a few days in our National Parks. Go to any of our major parks and you will see people drunk, smoking and throwing cigarette butts and matches, eating junk food and throwing plastic wrappers anywhere, blaring radios and music from all kinds of devices, shouting and behaving in ways that can leave one in no doubt that the humans didn't descend from monkeys. If they had, they would behave like monkeys, with respect and sensitivity to others who share the forest with them. Darwin would have changed his mind if he had visited Dhikala in Corbett National Park. But how do you get local people involved and interested in forests and wildlife conservation?

What I believe will help hugely in more ways than one is to involve our High School and College youth in wildlife conservation. It is only when the young generations learn to appreciate nature that they will do what needs to be done to protect and preserve it. I spent my entire school and college time in the 1960's and 70's, in the forests of the Sahyadri Hill Range in what is today called the Kawal Tiger Reserve. I would go off to the farm of Mr. Venkat Rama Reddy on the bank of the Kadam River and spend my entire summer and winter holidays with him. No electricity, no telephone, no running water. Wake and sleep with the sun. I walked uncounted miles of animal tracks with my friend Shivaiyya, Uncle Rama's Gond tracker, fished, bathed and swam in the Kadam and Dotti Vagu Rivers and sat at innumerable waterholes, watching animals and birds come to drink water in the summer where water is very scarce. As most of these rivers dry up in the summer, you can walk long distances on the river bed, where though the soft sand underfoot makes the going a little strenuous it saves you from the thorn bushes on the bank.

If you walk up in the Kadam streambed and turn right to go up the Dotti Vaagu, you would come to some deep pools in a very shaded spot. The water there does not dry out for a long time even in the summer. It is amazing how, as I write this today more than 45 years later, I can literally see in my mind the river, the pools, the bamboo fronds that cover that part of the forest, the light, and shade. I can still smell the forest on a sweltering hot afternoon and then the fresh smell of the earth in the morning, still wet with dewfall in the night. Memory is a powerful thing indeed. We didn't have cameras then, but we lived these beautiful times and the memory will stay with me for as long as I live. After that, who cares?

I recall vividly as if it were yesterday, one time when I was sitting in a blind that had been cut into the middle of an acacia thorn bush, about 30 feet up the bank of the Dotti Vaagu. Very cramped space, a log to sit on and a small space opened in the front of the bush to stick the barrel of the gun through to give me a clear shot, if some animal came to drink water. The bush itself was about 50 yards up the slope that borders the water hole. On this very hot summer day, this is the only source of water for miles around, left over dregs of Dotti Vaagu. When you sit silently, you become a part of the surroundings. Your ears initially buzz with the residual sound of the bustle you have left behind. But after a while, they fall silent and then you begin to hear the sounds of the forest. The buzzing of the cicadas, the incessant call of the Brain-fever bird, the distant barking of dogs from the village.

Then as your ears get more attuned to the sounds, you start hearing the subtler ones; the rustle of the leaves as a rat snake makes his way from one shaded spot to another, the cooing of the turtle doves, bark of the Chital sentry when she sees something alarming. You hear the breeze in the dry leaves on the forest floor as they play chase with each other. The teak trees having shed most of their leaves, the dominant color is brown. There is very little shade, except under the acacia thorns like the one I am sitting in. There is some bamboo, but most of it is young and does not provide shade. There are no elephants in this forest, but the Bison (Gaur) browse on what they can reach of the bamboo and so do the Chital, Sambar, and Nilgai.

As I keep sitting very still, even controlling my breathing, knowing that above all else it is movement that attracts attention and becomes visible, I suddenly see a pair of jackals materialize in front of me. The bitch is more cautious and is lagging behind. The dog is ahead. Both sense that something is perhaps not as it should be. However, the wind is blowing steadily in my face and so I know they can't smell me. The bitch even looks directly at me; perhaps she knows, maybe she can sense the rise and fall of my chest as I breathe or maybe it is an old memory she is trying to place. The moment passes and she follows her mate into the open. First, they drink, then they sit in the water on the edge and cool off in the intense heat of the day, then they start playing, chasing each other around like little puppies, secure in the knowledge that they are alone. It is a very rare moment for me, to be observing animals doing what they do when they are not afraid.

Even if I had a video camera, it could never capture the entire atmosphere; the excitement, the challenge of sitting silent and still like a tree stump, my outline broken by the bush I am sitting inside. The memory of those jackals is still so vivid in my mind that even today, 45 years later, I can see them playing in and around the water. Nothing lives that long in the wild. That pair of jackals is long gone. But I will remember them and that day, all my life.

After a while I realize that the jackals are a mixed blessing. Their presence will allay the fears of other animals heading to the water, as it is an indication that all is well. But at the same time, it will keep the smaller game, the Chinkara, the Chowsinga, and the Black-naped Hare away from the water hole. I want to make them leave but without alarming them so much that they warn everyone else of my presence. I gently clear my throat. It is as if an electric shock goes through their bodies. One minute they are carefree playmates. The next instant they go rigid for a split second and then like a flash, they are gone, each in a different direction to confuse the pursuer. I settle once again into the ritual of watching life happen. This enforced immobility and silence, the attendant boredom, initially; then the flow of thoughts in the mind, while trying to keep aware of the surroundings, is an incredibly powerful exercise for introspection. And waiting for and watching animals on a watering hole is the best way to do it.

I have not seen any initiative in our schools and colleges to encourage youth to spend time in the forests, not zipping around in Gypsies but actually camping and walking. They have no idea of the joy of waking up and watching the dawn breaking at the edge of a lake, waiting for the flights of duck and in season, geese to start coming over the horizon. I recall the incredibly beautiful magic of these flights, in V-formation come from one side before the rising sun, 'disappear' into it and then reappear on the other side as if they came out of the sun itself. As you watch the flights, you can hear fish plop in the water in the early morning feeding frenzy. They have no idea of the joy of listening to Cheetal alarm calls, asking a question and Sambhar answering it. That is when you understand the meaning of the term, 'Silence speaks louder than words'. Because if a Sambhar doesn't confirm the Cheetal's sighting, I for one, would put it down to the Cheetal's natural skittish nature of taking alarm at every shadow. I think this is the key to conservation, get the youth involved.

As the sunlight strengthens, the bird calls start. Invariably it is the Jungle Fowl rooster who calls first; his call that ends in a question. If you look for him, you will find him on any small rock or dry tree branch rising out of the wet morning forest floor, that catches the first rays of the rising sun. A little later the Peafowl call out their very loud and raucous bugles. The Langur sentinel alerts the jungle to the fact that he is awake and watching.

The problem is that today parents and teachers don't know the joy of spending time in a forest, so they can't teach others. Also, since they never learnt how to live in a forest, they are afraid and don't enjoy it. It is a vicious spiral. The love of the forest must be inculcated early in childhood through controlled experiences which are monitored to ensure safety and are essentially immersion learning classes in life skills. If we do it right, then I believe that we will create a generation that truly loves the wild places and will invest time, energy and resources to ensure that they remain unspoilt for future generations. This will also bring about a better understanding of matters critical to survival like Global Warming, which currently seems to be suffering from the problem of having been defined in a way that makes it almost impossible for the average city dweller who thinks that his eggs and milk come from the supermarket, to comprehend, much less relate to in a personal way.

I suggest that the government starts a program like the NCC (National Cadet Core) which we have in most schools and colleges. A National Forest Core (NFC) can be formed which can be run by the Forest Department (Wildlife Conservation Wing) which can hold jungle camps, seminars, photography lessons and contests and wildlife tracking and spotting activities in school holidays. All these can be self-financed, paid for by the children as they are excellent educational and leadership development activities. In these camps in addition to learning about nature, flora and fauna, they can be taught orienteering, survival skills, camping, tracking and photography. These camps must be held inside forests and Forest Guards must be involved in them. They can talk to the children, tell them stories of their encounters with wildlife and teach them the basics of being safe in a forest. They can take small groups of children and their teachers on nature walks where they can experience the forest. Walk to a lake and sit quietly on the bank, just inside the tree line and sketch the scenery. As they sit there, they can watch animals and birds that come to the lake and observe their behavior and try to identify them. What can be done on such outings is endless and beyond the scope of this article. I just want to give you a taste so that you will be motivated to take action.

What is more important is that children will learn to appreciate and love nature and the natural world and understand how much quality it adds to life and how much we need it. They will meet tribal people (Adivasis) and learn about their lives, stay with them, understand their problems and learn to empathize with them. They will learn the importance of the many cycles of life and death that take place in the forest, where everything that dies, gives life to something else. They will be detoxified and experience what it means to breathe fresh air where it is made; in forests. They will remember the sight of the night sky above them and see the millions of stars that they can never see in their cities. They will learn to enjoy silence, punctuated by sounds, each of them evidence of life and activity. They will take away with them, memories which will last them their lifetimes and remind them of what they owe the earth.

The Forest Department can give children who participate in these programs, Honorary Forest Guard badges and a National Park Membership card which will entitle them to concessional fees when they visit any National Park in the country. They can hold competitions, quizzes and practical challenge competitions and give prizes. The first prize could be a badge making that child, Honorary Wildlife Warden. Children who have been to several camps could be recruited to participate in the Annual Wildlife Census that happens in all parks. They will be energetic, enthusiastic and incorruptible and not likely to write numbers of tigers and leopards in census forms, while imbibing tea in the village.

What better way to spend the holidays camping out in forests, walking the earth and learning about those who we share the earth with?

Zoo in Corbett – Really?

LET ME INTRODUCE you to the tiger. He is not an animal. He is not a spectacle. He does not exist for your pleasure or like all politicians, for photo ops. He is not living in your land, you are encroaching on his. The tiger (gender neutral term as it refers to the species, and not to the male alone) is a meter. It is a meter that tells the tale of the health of the forest. Which translates to the health of the earth. Yes, the same earth which we call 'Mother'. The same earth of which there is only one and none other. The same earth on which we live, believe it or not, along with other species which are, again believe it or not, equally critical to the health and survival of the earth. Sorry. I apologize. Not equally critical but simply critical. And that is because they are, all of them, included in the list of those that are not destructive and toxic to the earth. If I made a comparative list of species comparing those that are consciously toxic to the health of the earth and those that are not, it would be a very simple matter. On one side – NOT TOXIC – I could list every living being of every imaginable kind. And on the other side, in solitary splendid disgrace, I would write – MANKIND. It looks like while introducing the tiger, I also introduced myself. Any resemblance to you is purely coincidental.

The tiger is a meter because it sits on top of the pyramid that constitutes the forest. At the bottom is the leaf mulch, molds and decomposing matter which produces the lifegiving nitrogen that powers all plant and tree growth. Trees produce oxygen. I wish they produced Wi-Fi also so that they wouldn't be cut down so fast. Trees provide cover to the earth and those who live on it. They prevent soil washing off in torrential rain. Trees are the world of insects, reptiles and birds. Trees are the foundation of their lives. They live on trees, eat off them, protect them, and are protected and given refuge by trees. And when they die, they provide the manure that trees live off. Trees also regulate temperature and rain.

In a healthy forest, there are healthy trees, which provide ground cover for herbivores, browsers and grazers, whose dung and eventually their bodies support tree growth. Herbivores breed profusely and frequently so their populations can decimate their own food supply. Some have large litters, others breed at least once a year, sometimes twice. Their young mature in months, not years. Herbivore population is therefore regulated by carnivores, leopards, wolves, hyenas and others with the apex predator, the tiger at the peak of the pyramid. They kill and eat the old, sick and weak and so ensure the overall health and breeding vigor of herbivores.

Carnivore population is self-regulated by longer gestation periods, one or two cubs which are mother dependent for up to two years and so the mother can't breed until her cubs are weaned. Cubs learn to hunt from their mothers and if the mother dies while they are still too young and have not learnt to hunt, they will perish. More carnivore mothers, especially the cats, leopards and tigers, have trouble rearing more than two cubs, sometimes even more than one. The others, even if they are born, perish. When carnivore populations grow, it indicates that herbivore populations are proliferating, which means that there is enough for them to eat which in turn indicates a healthy forest. It is a beautiful cycle. When carnivore population are artificially reduced by trapping and poaching and when herbivore populations are threatened by competition for grazing land from village cattle and the threat of disease that they bring into the forest, it means a threat to this whole cycle which in turn can mean a threat to the environment, which in its final stage, leads to death of forests, creation of deserts, reduction of rainfall, drying up of rivers and the death of humans. I hate to use self-interest as the argument in favor of protecting the environment but in a society where selfishness has been granted primary virtue status, what else can I do?

The tiger therefore is not an object of interest or a curiosity, but the single, most powerful indicator of our own future. I understand that our government in its own wisdom has decided to build a zoo in Corbett National Park, our primary tiger reserve to enable those who lack patience and don't care about the environment or forests or about anyone or anything that lives in them but still want to see a tiger. Typically, this means that the tiger, for no fault of his own, will be sentenced not just to life imprisonment, but to endless torture while it lives, so that the idle curiosity of gawkers can be satisfied. Is this something that you would like to support?

Why do I call it life imprisonment and endless torture? See for yourself. Once a tiger is caught and put into a cage (don't worry, being stuck on a tiny man-made island surrounded by a water filled moat is still a cage), it can never return to the wild. It would have lost all its fear of humans and developed an abiding hatred for them and so would be too dangerous to release in any forest.

The fact that it wasn't dangerous to begin with and became dangerous because of what we did to it, is neither here nor there. Endless torture because the tiger is a free roaming animal with a range of up to thirty square miles. It is territorial and doesn't like others encroaching on its territory. It is a solitary creature which likes to be left alone. It doesn't bother you if you don't bother it. I am living proof of this. Since I was fifteen, I have slept more times than I can recall, in dry stream beds and under massive trees in cool shade in prime tiger country and I am here, writing this article in defence of my friends (tigers) who decided not to eat junk food (me). On at least one occasion, I walked past a cave, half-way up a small rocky hillock in the Sahyadri Hills in Kadam forest (now the Kaval Tiger Reserve), in which a tigress had her infant cubs. She merely sat at the mouth of the cave and watched, as Shivaiyya, my Gond partner and I, walked past. I say, 'on at least one occasion', because that is the one I know about. Who knows how many other times I would have walked past a tiger or a tiger walked past me when I was asleep and left me alone?

Imagine this creature, used to square miles, confined in square feet and then harassed day and night by screaming, bleating and laughing humans, calling out to it while taking selfies. I sincerely hope that you can see how torturous it would be. To top it all, the poor tiger committed no crime to deserve this. Its crime is that it exists. Add to this, that the tiger, so confined is out of both the gene pool in the forest and unable to impact the life cycle that needs it, all because you wish to satisfy idle curiosity and you have added insult to injury, causing damage not just to one animal but to the future of the forest itself and all those that live in it.

What is the solution?

Educate people. Start with school children. Tell them the story of the tiger. Teach them woodcraft so that they can go into forests with knowledge, concern and commitment to life and enjoy the whole forest, not only search for tigers. I believe that the future of our planet lies in educating our youngsters so that they can appreciate nature without the need to change it and recast it in their own image. They must be taught to respect plants, animals, birds and insects, not only those which are 'beautiful' by our standards, but which are incredibly beautiful in their form and function as a sign of their Creator.

If you can't or won't do this, then please print out this picture, enlarge it and erect cutouts of this in all villages and cities of India, so that gawkers can gawk at the tiger from the comfort of their beds. Leave real, live tigers alone to live in peace and do what they were created to do; protect the earth and sustain life. Not torture and destroy it.

Come to the Okavango

FIRST THERE WAS the dry. Then it rained high up and far away in the mountains. And water flowed. Life giving water filled the river banks and overflowed. Life giving water which itself gives up its life in a few months when it sinks into the sands of the Kalahari Desert. But while it lasted, it would be called by a name that echoes in the halls of fame which list the most beautiful places on earth – the Okavango Delta.

For those who want to read more about this wonderful place, click below:

https://en.wikipedia.org/wiki/Okavango_Delta

It is like my arm – our guide and boatman, Happy – told us, talking about its shape. Rain falls on the shoulder, the mountains in Angola and water flows down the arm and into the fingers only to be swallowed up by the sands of the Kalahari, home, among other species, to the magnificent black-maned Kalahari lions. But while it lasts, the water gives life to an entire ecosystem of plants and resident and migrant animals and birds, that has no parallel on earth.

Our boatman introduced himself, 'I am Happy.'

I said, 'So am I.'

He said, 'That is my name.'

I said, 'That is my state.'

He gave up but first he smiled. The famous African smile, which the people of Botswana, the Batswana (Tswana people speaking Setwsana) seem to represent so well. A smile that starts in the heart and spreads all over the body and shines out of the face. When the man is happy you can see that in every part of his body. Not like the smile that is on the lips but the eyes say something else. If I could get reincarnated, I would wish to return as a boatman on the Okavango.

We landed in Maun; my dear brothers, Ebrahim Patel and Farouk Hassan and my mentor and teacher, Prof. Salman Nadvi. We had never heard of Maun but there it was, nevertheless, proving that whether people know you or not is a mark of their knowledge or lack of it; not a reflection on your significance. Maun has a wonderful little airport batting way above the average. The immigration official was anything but officious. He also had the trademark smile. Asked me how many days I wanted. I said, 'Five'. He said, 'I will give you ten.' I thanked him. On my return on the fifth day, he was again at the desk. I said to him, 'You gave me five days but I wish I had stayed for ten.' He said to me, 'Next time you must stay for ten. But I will give you twenty. Whatever you ask me for, I will give you more.' That seems to me to be the attitude of the people of Botswana. Such warm and lovely people.

We walked around our hired car with the company representative inspecting the car and found two scratches on one side. I helpfully offered to add two more on the other, if the man wished, but he emphatically refused my offer. And so, we drove off to the resort where we had booked our accommodation, The Thamalakane River Lodge. I have always wondered why African languages sound so musical. The most mundane word sounds lilting. I think it has to do with the fact that almost every word has three syllables. When you have three syllables, it makes it sound like a song. Thamalakane is not pronounced as it is written but as Tha-ma-la-ka-nay.

We were checked in by a very charming lady with once again a huge smile on her face and shown to our chalets which came with all amenities and a sign outside the door which read, 'Beware of hippos and crocodiles.' That was just in case you forgot that you were in Africa in the Okavango Delta. I don't know about wandering crocs but I heard a hippo loud and clear late one night. So, the sign was not for scenic effect alone. One 'amenity' that the chalets have, is a four-foot-high curving wall between the bedroom and bathroom. Nothing more. The resultant potential for auditory and olfactory sensations is impressive, to say the least. One is well-advised not to eat too many baked beans or peanuts for fear of replicating the sound effects of the Battle of the Bulge. This is a classic example of design before utility, even before common sense which not only takes away useable space from the bedroom but also ensures an assault on the senses that one can well do without. There is a point to be made about privacy and that intimacy needs to be limited within boundaries. Listening (and more) to your room partner (no matter your relationship with them) discharging their responsibilities is not an experience to be sought.

The first morning we were scheduled to go to Moremi Game Reserve http://www.moremigamereserve.com/

This is entirely inside the Okavango and has an area of 5000 square kilometers, which gives you an idea of how big the Okavango is. After the rains, it becomes totally water bound and most parts can't be reached overland. But when we went, though there had been rains, it was motorable. We got into our open Land Cruiser (the workhorse of Africa) and drove out of our lodge. Conversationally, Farouk Bhai asked the ranger driving the vehicle, 'How far is Moremi?' He said, '160 km to the gate.' That is when it struck me that sitting in a fast-moving open safari vehicle was not the most comfortable way to travel. What we should have done is to have driven in our hired car to the gate and then boarded the safari vehicle at the gate. Hindsight is always 20:20. Meanwhile we had a freezing cold drive ahead.

Driving through rural Botswana is different from driving through rural South Africa. South Africa has more developed infrastructure, better roads, electricity and more upmarket cars on the roads. There seem to be no speed limits but speed is limited by the road. Occasionally you do see a police car and I understand that you can be stopped for overspeeding. Botswanan Police have a very admirable reputation. Unlike the police in many other countries including mine, Botswanan Police strangely seem to think that the law is not open to interpretation, especially interpretation that is sought to be facilitated by the transfer of wealth from one pocket into another. Anyone who is stopped for a misdemeanor in Botswana had better come clean and quietly pay the fine unless he is seeking state hospitality. Going by the standards of Botswanan hospitality and the soft and easy going nature of the Tswana people, I dare say that may not be an end to be feared, but I would rather pay for my keep rather than the other way around. All this by way of filing-in color. We didn't meet any police nor did we need to seek state hospitality.

Why do roads get corrugated? This one was. Driving fast on a corrugated road is a hard-core way to get a vibrator massage. At the end of 160 km, my bones, teeth and brain were all rattling. Driving slowly makes it much worse so driving fast, it had to be. Once you get used to the cold wind in your eyes and your eyes have wept enough tears, your sight clears and you see small holdings on either side of the road. Small homes with large yards, filled with country chickens, ducks, turkeys and goats. There are cattle everywhere and horses and more donkeys than I have ever seen except in parliaments. And like those, these are also jealously guarded. I was told that the worst crime on a Botswanan road is to knock a donkey. But thankfully given their lethargy and contentment with their side of the fence, the chances of knocking one are negligible unless you set out to do this because you have a grudge against a particular donkey. Where there are horses and donkeys are also mules. Every single animal of every kind in top condition. That is what hits you first. Sleek, well cared for animals, well fed and well kept. I didn't see a single animal out of condition in all the many hundreds of kilometers we drove in that area.

The area is designated Code Red, meaning that it is susceptible to rinderpest, a dreaded cattle disease that is transmitted by the Cape Buffalo which are in the forests. As such there are fences to keep them there and not allow them to wander into inhabited areas. But fences are fences and buffalo are buffalo and the inevitable happens. What being in the Code Red area means is that beef produced in this area must be consumed in this area itself and can't be transported out of the area. This is done to prevent the spread of rinderpest to other parts of the country. Not a very happy prospect if you are a beef cattle farmer in this area but that is how it is.

In Moremi, what we saw lots of were single male elephants. Some in Musth, with the telltale secretions from the glands behind the ear as well as discolored hindlegs thanks to their almost constant urinating in this period. An elephant in Musth is not someone you want to meet, up close. And we didn't. But they were a magnificent sight with massive tusks. One had a couple of other males as companions; an old bull with two Askaris (guards). Another one was bathing and got disturbed when we turned up and flared his ears and shook his head to express his opinion. Another was busy digging for water in a waterhole that was damp but has no water in it. "But where are the herds?", I asked the ranger. Further inside the reserve, was his guess. Lots of Mopani trees, favorite elephant food, on both sides of the cattle fence that I mentioned above. However, inside the fence they are all cropped short as if by a hedge cutter. While outside the fence they grow tall and shady. Evidence of the attention of elephants which eat all new growth and so the tree never grows tall where there are elephant herds feeding on them. You can see this in Kruger National Park also;

hundreds of acres of neatly cropped Mopani. Wonderful creatures, elephants. My favorite among the Big Five.

In Moremi we also saw the Tsessebe antelope, the fastest of all African antelopes, very rare in the Kruger but much more common here; a giraffe making faces at us and ostriches with their superior looks down the nose.

We stopped for a picnic lunch on the bank of a lake, under some sausage trees. These have a gourd fruit which is like a very long and fat sausage. The fruit is supposed to have legendary properties related to human reproduction which I am sure you can guess. If you can't, then rejoice at the fact that you have a clean mind. The alleged properties are purely legendary and fictitious, so not to worry. What is more interesting about these trees is that it is from their trunks that the famous Mokoro (a dugout canoe) of the Okavango is made.

You must be brave and suicidal in equal measure to sit in a Mokoro in a place that is populated by hippos and monster crocs, but people do. Mokoro are the most common means of travel for local people and for tourists who go camping on the islands of the Okavango. Today, the government has prohibited the cutting of sausage trees to make canoes and so Mokoro are made of fiberglass. But you can still find plenty of authentic wooden Mokoro if you wish to take a ride. The boatman stands and poles it like the Shikara boatmen of Kashmir or the Gondolas of Venice, with the exception that in those places, you are not likely to meet a resident hippo with territorial tendencies or a sovereign citizen Nile Croc. Not an encounter to be wished for.

As we drove off, I spotted a Pied Lapwing; sitting on eggs in her nest and refused to move even when the wheels of the Land Cruiser were inches away. It simplly sat still like a statue, which is its most common defence against predators. If that fails, then it will take off and pretend that one wing is broken and goes away from the nest, calling plaintively until it has succeeded in drawing the predator far away from the nest, before it flies away. Then it makes a series of dive attacks on the predator until it drives it away completely. It is amazing to see how this small bird with almost nothing to defend itself, makes up for that in spirit and courage.

The next day we took an all-day boat ride, a flat-bottomed aluminum boat powered by an outboard motor, Happy at the wheel, and went up into the Okavango for over 150 kilometers. Imagine water so clean that you can see the bottom clearly 3-4 meters below, carpeted by multicolored lilies as far as the eye can see. Not a single plastic bag or piece of paper or cigarette to mar the landscape in hundreds of miles of wilderness. African Jacanas abound and wait until your boat is almost on them and then take off in low flight with their long stick-like legs and elongated web-less feet trailing behind. Imagine heaven or come to the Okavango.

As you proceed, you will see the eyes and snout of a hippo bull staking out his territory. If you get too close, he will dive and can remain underwater for over half an hour. Usually he will surface a distance away and face you again. When you are in a motorboat this is an interesting sight. In a Mokoro, you don't want to see it. For if he decides that you are a threat, he can submerge and surface under you and give you a very real chance at becoming a historical figure. Hippos kill more people annually in Africa than all other animals combined, so they are a real threat, not be scoffed at.

Lots of birds in the Okavango of which African Fish Eagles with their striking plumage, white head, neck and a bib on the chest, stand out miles away. If there is a tall tree, you can rest assured that you will find an African Fish Eagle on it, scanning all around for prey. The other very common bird is the African Jacana, busily walking on water – actually, running on its especially adapted feet on the lily pads which cover almost all open water in the Okavango. You will see all species of Kingfisher but the black and white, Pied Kingfisher seems to be the most common.

Then there are Egyptian geese, sunning themselves close to a huge crocodile. Plenty of Nile Crocodiles in this place, some of them real monsters.

Imagine driving through a narrow channel through head-high reedbeds where you can't see on either side anything except impenetrable reeds, waving in the breeze. The reed beds give way once again to lily carpets interspersed with islands. These islands are mostly the result of birds depositing seeds on termite mounds. Here is a very interesting account of how these islands are formed. http://www.itravelto.com/okavango-islands.html

The islands are home to wildlife, Lechwee antelope, elephant, hippo, lions, leopard and in some places, cheetah. Warthog and other smaller game like jackals, hyena and occasionally wild dog also inhabit the islands. As the day progresses and the sun comes out, you are likely to see crocodiles sunning themselves on the edges of islands, always within reach of the water, to slide into at the slightest hint of danger. Although looking at some of the monsters, you can see that nothing except humans are any danger to them. These islands range in size from literally termite mounds to vast tracts of land, the biggest of them being Chief's Island. This used to be the private hunting reserve of the tribal chief and is now a thriving tourist hub. You can fly in to Chief's Island from Maun or drive there or take a boat.

Sitting in the bow of our boat, with the wind blowing through my fast disappearing hair, I couldn't but think of the prospect of meeting another boat traveling in the opposite direction at the same speed. Quite likely and scary especially around the many bends. Even less happy is the thought of being in a Mokoro and meeting a boat like this come at you round a bend. The problem is that even if the boatman stops his boat, which happens quite easily because given the resistance of water, if he throttles down, the boat comes to a halt; the bow wave that it creates, doesn't stop with the boat. A motorboat traveling fast, can create a wave big enough to completely swamp and sink a Mokoro. As I said, not a happy thought.

We stop at an island for lunch, only to discover that the hotel has packed us non-halal food. That is when we discover how little we really need to eat. One apple each and a small packet of chips, washed down with water. Happy is very unhappy with this development and the hotel's failure and promises to take up the issue with them while proceeding to demolish our nonshariah compatible chicken et al. All at our invitation of course. No point in wasting food, is there?

Sitting on the 'beach' of the island (which Happy said was about 10 sq km in size) watching the Okavango Delta before us, I could only marvel at the cycle of beginning and end that the delta represents. From the dry season when it is desert, to the wet, when it is a sea of water giving life to many. Then a few months later the water sinks into the sand once again to repeat the cycle once again. Our 'lunch' finished, we get back on board the boat once again to resume our journey back to the Thamalakane River Lodge.

Water everywhere with lilies now preparing to shut shop for the night. The hippo's grunting roar as we pass, a greeting or warning, as you may like to interpret it. A Saddle-billed stork, stalking his way back from the water's edge. Lots of Letchwee antelopes, horned males with their harems. They used to be called Red Letchwee but I understand they have been renamed, Common Antelope, a development to which I am sure they would take exception if they knew. But it gives you an idea about their numbers.

As we progress, the sun which has been traveling its course, finally extinguishes itself in the waters of the Delta, but not before giving us a final spectacular display of orange and red. A new display every day that changes minute by minute. Never to be repeated. Infinite variety to delight the senses and draw the mind to the Creator of it all.

The Okavango is a place to be visited again and again and never to be forgotten.

For all my photos of the Okavango and Moremi, please go to: https://goo.gl/photos/DDNkJNyxE6CqfyRW6

Corbett Park Tourism

THE INDIA TOURISM byline is - Incredible India.

I agree. I encountered it. Here is what happened.

I decided to go to Corbett Tiger Reserve - being one of my favourite places on earth. I am a lifelong wildlife enthusiast and photographer and ensure that I spend at least a few days every quarter in the wilds. There are sea people, mountain people and among the Arabs - desert people. I am a forest person. Nothing gives me greater pleasure than to spend time by myself, without any connection to the outside world, in the middle of a forest.

Having done this all my life, I consider myself to be fairly knowledgeable about the sounds and signs of the jungle and know how to read them so that I keep myself safe from danger while enjoying the beauty of unspoilt nature. In the world that I grew up in, all I needed to do was to take a small haversack and catch a bus and a few hours later I would be in the forests of the Aravalli hills, in the farm house of my dear friend and mentor, Venkat Rama Reddy sahib, located on the bank of the Kadam River in Adilabad district (Map link). But today I have to go to an official wildlife sanctuary and so am forced to come into contact with those denizens of the forest who are not listed in the list of wildlife that you are likely to encounter there. Therefore you are unprepared when you do encounter them. I thought I should do the kind thing and prepare you so that you are not caught unawares and pay the price of shattered dreams.

I started by taking the law abiding citizen route and tried to make a booking on the internet on the Corbett Tiger Reserve website which promises a lot. I had been to Dhikala and Bijrani Ranges in 2006 and so I decided to go to a different range and chose Sona Nadi Range. That range has three Forest Guest Houses. I had four days and decided to spend two in one guest house and two in another so that we would be able to see two different parts of the park. And that is where my story began:

I entered all the data that the form asks for and selected two days for Haldupudao guest house but the system would take only one day or three days. I wanted two. Then I thought I would be clever and book the two days, one by one. So I chose one day and completed the booking and made the payment with my credit card. Then I went in again to choose another day but the system wouldn't accept the booking claiming that I have visited the park less than one month ago. Since I last visited the park nine years ago, I was astonished. But to no avail. The system knew best and repeatedly rejected my booking for another day. So eventually in frustration I decided to cancel the booking I had already made as I didn't want to go from Hyderabad to Corbett for one day's stay. But the system refused to accept the cancellation. Imagine my further astonishment when this happened.

However, there were two numbers that I could call in case of difficulty, so I did. But I forgot, though being Indian I should have known better, that in Indian Government (Forest Department and Wildlife Sancturies are Government of India, believe me) if they say you can call, that is precisely what they mean. You can call. As many times as you like. There is on restriction on that. However, they didn't say that anyone would answer your call, did they? So how can you blame them if they don't? And that is what happened to me. I called and called and no answer. As they say, perseverance pays - though not always what you wish. So after the tenth call a lady answered in Hindi. I speak Hindi fluently so no problems there.

I explained my problem to her and asked if she could help.

Corbett Lady: Aap internet par booking keejiye. Hum kuch nahi kar saktay.

(You can book on the internet. We can't do anything)

Me: Madam main nay internet par hi booking kee hai. Wahan booking nahi ho rahi hai. Isi liye aap ko call kiya kyon ki aap ka number website par diya hai.

(Madam, I tried doing that and it is not working. That is why I called you because your number is given on the website)

Corbett Lady: Hum kuch nahin kar saktay. Aap internet par booking keejiye.

(You can book on the internet. We can't do anything)

Me: (after going this route a couple of times more) Achcha Madam aap hamari booking cancel kar deejiye aur payment reverse kar deejiye.

(Okay Madam, please cancel my booking and reverse the payment.)

Corbett Lady: Aap internet par booking keejiye. Hum kuch nahi kar saktay.

(You can book on the internet. We can't do anything)

Me: Madam booking cancel karnay ko kah raha hoon. Aap cancel karengi tho mujhe paisa wapas milega. Warna mera paisa nahin mil sakta. Please cancel keejiye.

(Madam, I am asking you to please cancel the booking and return my money. Unless you cancel the booking the credit card payment can't be reversed and I can't get my money back. Please cancel the booking, I request you.)

Corbett Lady: Nahin karengay.

Me. Madam, mera paisa hai. Meri booking hai. Aap ko sirf cancel karnay ko kaha. Kyon nahin karengay?

Corbett Lady: Nahin karengay.

(I won't do it.)

And she hung up.

Now I am the persistent sort and definitely dislike my money being stolen, no matter who does it. I pay my taxes diligently and see no reason to subsidize the government any more. So I used my connections and got a friend to help and had them make the booking for the other days in Ramnagar where the Corbett Park Head Quarters are located. But thanks to some more communication issues, all four days got booked in Haldupudao guest house.

I didn't have the energy to make any more changes and so left it like that. Corbett is beautiful and if I had to stay in one guest house for four days, so be it. At Ramnagar we took our Gypsy safari vehicle and proceeded to Haldupudao. We arrived at the Vatanvasa gate and when I gave my booking (called permit) to the guard, I realized that the permit was printed in English while the Forest Guards at the gate didn't have a word of it. So I had to translate for them. I could have said whatever I wanted of course and they had no means of knowing if I spoke the truth but I did speak the truth and translated properly wondering what the point of a permit in English was, when it was to be read by people who don't speak the language at all.

It takes roughly three hours to get to Haldupudao but since most of that journey is through the forest, crossing rivers on wooden bridges and driving over gravel river beds with a foot or more of water, it was thoroughly enjoyable. The Maruti Gypsy is the vehicle of choice for Indian jungle roads. It has front wheel drive, and FWD if you need it and does everything except climb trees.

Our driver has to be one of the most service oriented guys I have ever met. He is employed by a local tour operator and so is uninfected with Sarkaari Jaraseem (Official Germs). He is a very skilled driver and a cook rolled into one, speaks Hindi like a runaway express train and is full of great wisdom like what he said about our current times:

Ghoday ko na milay ghaas par Gadhe khayen Chawanprash

We arrived in Haldupudao and as we drove in I was delighted to see the guest house, an old stone bungalow (built in 1849) with its typical wide veranda in front and chimneys promising a fire place in the house. There is nothing more enjoyable than a log fire in the sitting room on a cold winter night and nothing more painful than its absence. But to my surprise we didn't go to the guest house but to what was the Outhouse (a plaque still states that) upon which had been built two rooms with bathrooms. The problem was that there were twenty high stairs to get to them. I had a bad knee and my doctor strictly forbade climbing stairs. Nowhere in the booking process did it say anything about stairs. So what was I to do?

(That's a picture of me struggling up the stairs)

I tried speaking to the care taker about this:

Me: Hum us guest house mein nahin reh saktay hain?

(Can't we stay in that (old) guest house)

CT: Nahin Saab

(No Sir)

Me: Kyon?

(Why?)

CT: Wo sirf Wan Adhikarion kay liye hai

(That is only for Forest Authorities)

Me: Tho kya koi aanay wala hai in char dinon mein?

(Is any of them booked to come here during the next four days)

CT: Nahin Saab

(No Sir)

Me: Tho phir hum kyon nahin reh saktay hain?

(Then why can't we stay there?)

CT: Kyon ki aap Wan Adhikaari nahin ho.

(Because you are not a Forest Authority)

That was plain enough even for my stupid head. That's how our bureaucracy, strangely called Civil Service (which is neither civil nor a service) works. Gathers unto itself all that it has been given in trust.

So I abandoned that line and tried to appeal to his better self. But I should have first checked to see if it was with him. I discovered later that it was still in his village with his family. I am not reporting that conversation because it is simply too tedious. The long and short of it was that I had no option but to ignore my doctor and climbed up and down the stairs for four days, praying that I didn't end up suffering for it.

The night was fantastic as all nights in the forest are. There is a cook in Haldupudao who will cook what you bring. The cook believes that he can cook and he has the freedom to believe whatever he likes as this is a free country. However, if it hadn't been for the culinary skills of our driver, we would have been captive victims of his cooking and lucky to escape with our lives. As it was, the cook became our guest and ate better than he would have fed anyone. He was a man with spiritual inclination and so every night after dinner he would be in his cups and we would be his captive audience, listening to his caterwauling from the lower floor as we tried to sleep upstairs. Mercifully his stamina didn't keep up with his spirits and he shortly fell asleep and left us to do the same.

The rooms we occupied didn't have heating or a fireplace to light a fire in and so on the first night I froze to death. My feet lost contact with me and I tried to imagine how I would manage without feet the next day. Truly it is said that necessity is the mother of invention and so the cold forced me to invent the hot water bottle. I took two plastic water bottles, filled them with boiling water and inserted them under my blanket praying they wouldn't burst. They didn't and I slept well the next two days. By the morning, 5.00 a.m. however they get cold and so getting up and washing in cold water which appeared to come straight from a glacier was decidedly painful.

The highlight of the first night was that at about 4.00 a.m. I heard the alarm call of a Barking Deer from right inside our camp. He was calling so insistently that I was sure there was a leopard outside the door. So I quietly got out of bed and opened my door and came out on the landing to be greeted with the sight of a female leopard that had come calling. She sat on her haunches like a dog and looked up at me and I looked down at her. Then she got up and walked away, evidently not liking what she saw. Rejection is painful, even by a female leopard.

Next morning, we started out early as that is the best time to see predators – tigers and leopards. It was very misty and bitterly cold and an open Gypsy is not the best place to be in at that time. But off we went, wrapped in garment after garment, trying to prove the efficacy of layering to keep the cold out. We drove down one road and watched the sun rise over the river. Absolutely beautiful sight. Then we drove back a ways and tried to go on another road because we had not seen anything on the road we went on first. To our surprise but not delight we found that road closed. Our driver took us to another road and we drove up that for a bit and encountered another road block. So in effect, three out of four roads were blocked.

We returned for breakfast and I asked the Forest Department Official who stays in Haldupudao about the roads. He said that repairs were being done to bridges and so the roads were closed. I asked him why in that case, this was not mentioned on the website or why this location was not closed for bookings until the roads were useable. He shrugged. Such an expressive gesture, the shrug. Done well, it can mean anything at all. And what's more it leaves you to decide what you want it to mean. I decided that I wanted it to mean end of conversation and reminded myself of my own quote – I will not allow what's not in my control to prevent me from doing what is in my control. It was in my control to enjoy myself. It was not in my control to teach the Forest Department the fundamentals of customer service. So I was going to leave what was not in my control and do what was in my control and enjoy myself notwithstanding.

We drove up and down that one road for four days. We saw trees, termite mounds that were the epitome of industry and could be inspirations of architects.

We saw more trees and a very ambitious Kingfisher out of touch with reality who had caught a fish bigger than his head and so couldn't swallow it. We saw even more trees and otters catching fish and then peeping at us over boulders in the river, their curiosity getting the better of them but so beautifully camouflaged that it was almost impossible to see them. We saw Chital grazing and late one evening and suddenly a Chital hind started stamping her foot and sounding her alarm and gazing intently at a thicket in which was a predator, which didn't show himself to us. We saw a Sambar stag in repose and several Barking Deer, always alarmed at life. But we saw no tigers in

Corbett Tiger Reserve. Nor did we see any elephants though we saw tiger pug marks and elephant dung to our heart's content. I believe this was because we couldn't really explore the area that was given to us because roads were closed but nobody bothered to inform us.

Nobody can guarantee any sightings, especially of tigers and leopards which are nocturnal animals and shy to boot but if there are enough opportunities to roam the forest, then the chances of sighting increase dramatically. That is what wildlife tourism is supposed to do – increase your chances of seeing the animals. And that is what we were denied because roads were closed.

In short, I am convinced that Corbett is a lovely place but the people in charge are decidedly strange. Their idea of customer service is the same as how they pronounce the word CUSTOMER – KASHT MAR. Ya'ani – Kasht say mar.

Incredible India indeed.

So, what's the solution?

Quite simple really. Let the Forest Department deal with the forest. And leave tourism to those who know how to treat people. Outsource tourism to a private company and let them pay a royalty to the Forest Department.

But will this happen? Incredible India once again.

Forest days and nights

ONE OF THE greatest needs today is for us, human beings, to get back in touch with nature. It is not our evil intent but our indifference, ignorance and disconnect that is the root cause behind global warming, environmental destruction, wildlife extinction, pollution of rivers and oceans and the consequent backlash to our own existence. If not altruism, then at least selfishness and the instinct for self-preservation should galvanize us to stop doing the things which will invariably and inexorably result in our own extinction. If we were to ask the animals, birds and insects; if we were to ask the fish in the ocean; they would all unanimously say that they are waiting for that day of extinction of the one species which had the greatest knowledge, gifts, material wealth and power, but which it used not to help others or even itself but to commit suicide while destroying the only home it will ever have. I sometimes imagine archeologists digging up the mounds of earth covering our cities with their great libraries, universities and laboratories and wonder how people who knew so much ignored that knowledge and did their best to destroy themselves, successfully.

That is why I believe that it is essential for us to get back in touch with nature, with the wild places on the earth; precious few that we have left; and with nature in every little way that is still with us in our own dwelling places. We need to learn the value of silence, of listening, of breathing fresh air and savoring the aromas it wafts to us and recognize them as the signatures of those who share this planet with us. I use the word, 'Share', very consciously because it is that attitude which must result from our encounter with nature. Sharing is the understanding that the other is co-owner with me. That I don't own it and the other doesn't enjoy it at my pleasure. Sharing is the true essence of citizenship; not of some nation state created by drawing lines on a map but of the earth, which we share with everyone else on it. To experience sharing is to experience respect for our fellow beings, human or otherwise.

Sadly, we have learnt to live as conquerors, despoilers, looters and exploiters of the earth. That is why we call climbing to the top of a great mountain, 'conquering' that mountain. If you could hear, you'd hear the mountain laugh its guts out at the audacity of mankind which pretends to conquer something that existed aeons before humans came into being and will continue aeons after the last of them has walked the plank. We carry this same attitude with respect to the rest of our fellow citizens, who we kill for commercial gain, for sport, or simply to sight our weapons; who we hook on a line and call their desperate death struggles – a good fight.

Ah@! Enough of that. Enough of lamenting. Let us see what we can do about it. How can we inculcate a love for nature, respect for it, appreciation of it, awareness of our own role; not as some conqueror; but as a small but important cog in the wheel of life. It is this love which leads me to the forest. It is this love that I want to transfer from my heart into yours.

To love the forest, you must learn to become a part of it. To feel, sense, listen, see and breathe like the wild things do. Buzzing around in 4X4 vehicles chasing animals, disturbing their peace, talking loudly, throwing out plastic litter, hanging out of the widows or over the sides taking pictures; all this despicable behavior must stop. To love the forest, you must walk in it. You must sit by a stream or waterhole, your outline broken by a bush and sit so still that even your breathing becomes invisible. Then the magic happens.

It was 1970. I was 15 years old, sitting in a blind that had been cut into the middle of a wild Ber thorn bush on the bank of a nameless tributary of Dotti Vaagu which in its turn is a tributary of River Kadam. Very cramped space, a log to sit on and a small space opened in the front of the bush to stick the barrel of the gun through to give me a clear shot, if some animal came to drink water. The bush itself was about 50 yards up the slope that borders the water hole. On this very hot summer day, this is the only source of water for miles around, left over dregs from the monsoon when this little trickle flowed bank to bank. It is summer, temperatures in the high 40's Celsius. In this part of the Sahyadri Range, it is so dry that you don't sweat. Or rather, the sweat dries so fast that you only see its white encrusted salt deposits in the armpits of your shirt when you take it off.

The breeze, when it blows, is a mixed blessing. On the one hand, the stillness is stifling, but on the other, when the breeze blows, it is like the blowback from a furnace. Well, not quite that bad but almost. However, what is wonderful and the reason I am waiting for it, is the smells it brings. If you spend enough time in the forest and have a good teacher to teach you to recognize sights, smells and sounds, it is like reading a book. You sniff the air and it tells you its own story.

There are many smells in the forest and they vary depending on the time of day and the time of year, the season. In the early morning in summer, it smells like first rain; the smell of dew from the previous night. Despite the heat of the day, night temperature drops 10 degrees or more and so there is often heavy dew fall. That nourishes whatever vegetation escaped being dried off by the sun and is the source of water for the hundreds even thousands of insects, reptile and even some mammal species in the forest. This moisture in the summer smells like first rain. Incidentally, in Hyderabad, our perfumers (Attar) had developed an Atar (perfume) called Gil, which means moist earth, based on the smell of first rain.

Depending on where you are, the breeze can bring to you the smell of the territory markings of a tiger, which urinates on specific trees, rocks and outcrops to warn off potential competitors. The strong smell of bovine urine can mean that there is or has been a Gaur (bison) herd in the vicinity. And depending on the forest, there is the smell of elephant. That is one smell you learn to recognize very early or you reach the point of no return. It is important to remember that animals can smell much more keenly than we can and so wearing after shave, perfume or even bathing with a perfumed soap can ensure that you never see a butterfly all day because animals smelt you a mile away and took another route. Same goes for tobacco, cigarettes, bidis and whatnot. I would bathe after my return from the forest in the night and go back the next morning without bathing. Sweat is natural and doesn't drive animals away.

When you sit silently, you become a part of the surroundings. Your ears initially buzz with the residual sound of the bustle you have left behind. But after a while, they fall silent and then you begin to hear the sounds of the forest. The buzzing of cicadas, the incessant call of the Brain-fever bird, the distant barking of dogs from the village.

Then as your ears get more attuned to the sounds, you start hearing the subtler ones; the rustle of leaves as a rat snake makes his way from one shaded spot to another, the cooing of turtle doves, bark of the Chital sentry when she sees something alarming. You hear the breeze in the dry leaves on the forest floor as they play chase with each other.

Teak trees having shed most of their leaves, the dominant color is brown. There is very little shade, except under the Ber and Acacia thorn bushes like the one I am sitting in. There is some bamboo, but most of it is young and does not provide shade. There are no elephants in this forest, but Gaur (bison) browse on what they can reach of the bamboo and so do Chital, Sambar, and Nilgai.

As I sit very still, even controlling my breathing, knowing that above all else it is movement that attracts attention and becomes visible, I suddenly see a pair of jackals materialize in front of me. The bitch is more cautious and is lagging behind. The dog is ahead. Both sense that something is perhaps not as it should be. However, the wind is blowing steadily in my face and so I know they can't smell me. The bitch even looks directly at me; perhaps she knows, maybe she can sense the rise and fall of my chest as I breathe or maybe it is an old memory she is trying to place. The moment passes and she follows her mate into the open. First, they drink, then they sit in the water on the edge and cool off in the intense heat of the day, then they start playing, chasing each other around like little puppies, secure in the knowledge that they are alone. It is a very rare moment for me, to be observing animals doing what they do when they are not afraid.

Even if I had a video camera, it could never capture the entire atmosphere; the excitement, the challenge of sitting silent and still like a tree stump, my outline broken by the bush I am sitting inside. The memory of those jackals is still so vivid in my mind that even today, more than 40 years later, I can see them playing in and around the water. Nothing lives that long in the wild. That pair of jackals is long gone. But I will remember them and that day, all my life.

After a while I realize that the jackals are a mixed blessing. Their presence will allay the fears of other animals heading to the water, as it is an indication that all is well. But at the same time their presence will keep the smaller game, Chinkara, Chowsinga, and Black-naped Hare away from the water hole. I want to make them leave but without alarming them so much that they warn everyone else of my presence. I gently clear my throat.

It is as if an electric shock goes through their bodies. One minute they are carefree playmates. The next instant they go rigid for a split second and then like a flash, they are gone, each in a different direction to confuse the pursuer. I settle once again into the ritual of watching life happen.

This enforced immobility and silence, the attendant boredom, initially; then the flow of thoughts in the mind, while trying to keep aware of the surroundings, is an incredibly powerful exercise for introspection. And waiting for and watching animals on a watering hole is the best way to do it.

Of game drives and choices

HE WAS THE KING of the forest (or so he thought about himself). He stood over five feet tall at the shoulder, weighed over one thousand pounds, with a massive neck supporting a rack of magnificent antlers rising high above that. The antlers were very impressive to look at and very useful in battle when he had to defend his harem against uppity youngsters, trying their strength against him. They could however be a fatal liability in thick bush as they could get caught in it and become the cause of his demise, if had to make a quick dash to save himself from his only predator, the tiger. So, he had learnt to stay in relatively open areas of rocky slopes, dotted with trees and some bush. He knew how to stand or sit with his outline broken so that to the casual observer he became a part of the landscape, his body color merging with the earth and his antlers simply dead branches. Especially when he was aware of being watched but not yet alarmed to make a dash for it, he knew how to be so still that even a second look wouldn't reveal him to the observer. What he had no control over was his ears. They had to keep moving to scan for sounds, which may spell danger from a direction he was not looking at. And they were what gave away his location to the observer who had patience. https://en.wikipedia.org/wiki/Sambar_deer

On this day, he had had good browsing all night and then just before dawn he had gone to his favorite rolling spot; a wide pool full of slush. His kind rolled in it until they were covered in liquid mud which later dried to form a coat impermeable to flies and biting insects which were the bane of his life. A good roll ensured that he would be able to rest up during the day peacefully. Sambar are active at and after dusk into the night and so spend most of the day, resting in shady spots. The only danger with rolling was that tigers also knew about this luxury of Sambars. So, rolling spots were a favorite ambush spot for the tiger. For the tiger, a Sambar rolling in the mud is almost a sure meal because it is impossible for the Sambar to rise from a prone position on his back and side and run before the tiger closes on him. So, Sambar are extremely cautious when they go to roll and spend far more time casing the joint, than in actually rolling. The roll is really a quick one, very like a horse rolling in the dust (for the same reason) and then he is up, all senses in high alert, trying to see if he can do another roll or must run for it.

For an animal this big, Sambar are extremely agile and gallop up and down steep rocky slopes as if they were flying. Having ridden horses, cross country I can vouch for it that there is no horse or horseman in the world which can chase a Sambar either up or down a slope without breaking a leg of the horse and killing himself. But Sambar do it all the time. As a matter of fact, their favorite escape tactic is to race downhill at full gallop, which even tigers can't match them at. All this of course if they are alert to danger and get as much of a head start as possible. Awareness is their best defence and their best guarantee of survival. This stag had reached his prime because he had mastered the art of being alert. There were deep claw marks on his withers to show the only encounter with a tiger; a young male whose ambition exceeded his ability. But still his claws drew lines in the Sambar stag's hide that healed but remained as a reminder to him of the importance of being on his guard all the time.

Today he had been sitting in the shade of a large, gnarled Babool tree halfway up the slope of the range of hills that rise from the waters of the Kadam Dam. After his browsing in the night, he had had a long and cool drink from the waters of the lake and climbed up the slope to his favorite spot under this tree. It was high enough to give him a vantage point. Before him was open land, very rocky and interspersed with stunted Seetaphal (Custard Apple), Lantana, Ber and young Babool. Behind him the hillside rose steeply and was covered with scree which meant that anyone coming down that slope would almost certainly send a few small stones rolling down, enough to alert him to possible danger. It was still fairly early in the day but it promised to be another hot one. Summers here tended to be extremely hot with temperatures in the forties. The sky was clear and blue which would take a steely hue as the sun racked up the temperature but for now, the breeze blowing his way over the water of the dam was still cool. All seemed right with the world but he was not happy. Something within him told him that today was not a day like all others. There was an ominous feeling inside him which he couldn't describe but which his kind had learnt to trust. A feeling of impending danger which he couldn't find evidence for but which he knew could save his life. He was uneasy but not yet alarmed enough to leave his cool spot in the shade and make a break for it.

I was nineteen years old and spending my summer vacation with Uncle Rama in Sethpally, a little village in Adilabad District of Telangana. Sethpally is close to the bank of the Kadam River which flows into the lake created by the Kadam Dam, from which rise the mountains of the Sahyadri Range. Rocky and sparsely covered with semideciduous forest and thorn bush but famous for Sambar. As it is open forest, the stags tend to grow a large head of antlers, a prime consideration for trophy hunters. The biggest stags are to be found further north in Madhya Pradesh, but the Sambar of this part of the world were nothing to be sneezed at either.

I used to spend all my vacations with Uncle Rama on his farmhouse which was on the bank of the Kadam wandering in the forest all day or if I was home, sleeping off the hottest part of the day in the thick shade of the three huge tamarind trees that grew between the farmhouse and the river. There is no air-conditioning to beat the coolness of the shade of a tamarind tree and no soothing sleep inducing music to beat the sound of the breeze rustling its leaves. The forest is never totally silent, though between midday and late afternoon, which is the hottest part of the day, is perhaps the quietest. Still you would hear the occasional barking of a dog from the Gond village on the other side of the river, or the cooing of Ring Necked doves roosting in the thick foliage of the tamarind trees I was sleeping under. Occasionally the alarm call of the Red Wattled Lapwing would sound its question, 'Did-you-do-it?' over and over until presumably it discovered who had done it. All this over the background of the ceaseless buzz of the Cicadas and the call of the Common Hawk Cuckoo (Brain Fever Bird), starting low and rising to a crescendo and ending only to rise again. Here is a recording of it: https://www.youtube.com/watch?v=bPqi5BcfETM But all these sounds are part of the atmosphere of the forest and not only don't disturb your sleep but soothe you into it. Today, over forty years later, I still remember the peace and tranquility of that sleep.

Last evening Uncle Rama decided that we should go on a game drive. Now these are things that I'd only known to have happened in British India with the Maharajas and their cronies the White Sahibs. To actually be one of the guns in a game drive is something that I had never imagined in my wildest dream. My excitement knew no bounds. I could hardly sleep that night. The next day there was a council of war, as it were. The head of the Lambada Tanda (Tanda is what a Lambada village is called) came to see Uncle Rama to decide on the number of men we would need for the drive.

Plans were made for camping as we would be away for three days in all. These were the days when hunting was permitted and so all permissions were obtained and the local DFO (District Forest Officer) was one of the invitees. My single thought, however, was to get a big Sambar stag to my credit.

The place we planned to go to was some miles away from the farm, a part of the Sahyadri Mountain Range (Western Ghats) that bordered the Kadam River dam. These hills are thickly forested and very steep, coming down to the water's edge on one side and rolling away, one into another on the other; ideal Sambar country. Also, ideal tiger and leopard country. The Sambar in this area is a large animal with the stags sporting a very respectable set of antlers, but not the gigantic racks of the Sambar of Madhya Pradesh. These are forest Sambar and an overly large head of horns would be a distinct disadvantage. Having said that, it is only in comparison that their antlers are smaller. By themselves they are very impressive indeed.

In addition to the species I mentioned, in these hills that we were going to beat, are wild boar, sloth bears, bison, and peacocks. No Chital or Nilgai as they prefer more open area. Also, many Grey Jungle Fowl with their familiar crowing in the mornings and at dusk. So, there was much expectation about all the different animals that we were likely to see. We had emphatic instructions from Uncle Rama that we were not to shoot a tiger, bear, bison, or leopard under any circumstances. Everything else was fair game. And the main quarry of course was a good Sambar stag. Shoot or not, the very thought that we would possibly see a tiger or leopard at close quarters was something to make the heart race in anticipation and not a little fear. As it happened, we did not see any of the 'prohibited' species.

But let me tell the tale in sequence for it is one in which I discovered something about myself. Something that I remember with happiness and pride to this day.

We started just before day break the next morning, having spent the greater part of the night in preparation. Guns to be cleaned, ammo to be sorted out and kept in order so that it was easily accessible. Food for the day plus cooking pots, condiments, some vegetables, rice, dal, sugar, tea, and milk powder for the next three days. Camping stuff; sleeping bags, small tents, and all the rest. And of course, knives. However, one major caveat –

the word 'knife' was not to be spoken aloud in any language. Uncle Rama believed that if one said the word 'knife' (in any language – as we all habitually spoke at least 3 languages) it would bring us bad luck and we would not see any game. So, we made very sure never to say 'knife'. Uncle Rama had a beauty, a medium sized switch blade knife with a tungsten steel blade, sharp as a razor. I was its keeper as I was also the official 'Halaal' guy, whose job it was to make sure that at least one of the animals shot was killed in the Muslim, zabiha way, so that I and Uncle Rama's other Muslim friends would not go hungry.

By the time we reached Kadam River Dam, it was getting light. We parked the jeeps by the canal and started off in a single file up the forest track. The Lambadas were already at the site and we had many willing hands for the stuff we were carrying. Each of us only carried his personal weapon. Uncle Rama was a great stickler for safety and made sure that there was no cartridge up the spout of any gun and that all safety catches were on. Silence was essential as we didn't want to disturb the game and it was prohibited to shoot anything on the way to the camp. We walked on as daylight grew stronger, harbinger of the heat of the day that was to come.

As we climbed the hills, I looked all around me hoping to see signs of the game that we had come to hunt. But apart from occasional droppings, there was not a sign that anything lived in these hills. The path wound serpentiously along through dry teak plantation forests, with the huge dry teak leaves crackling loudly if you stepped on them. This was almost impossible to avoid and it made me even more anxious that we were scaring all the animals away by our loud approach. Finally, at about 8:30

am we came to a clearing, a large expanse of open ground, very rocky and sloping down to the river on one side. All the trees in sight were dry and leafless so there was almost no shade and the sheet of rocks promised a very hot stay. However, we were not planning to stay in the tents that were pitched immediately and in any case, I was too excited to worry about anything other than the coming hunt.

After a hurried breakfast, and fortified by extremely sweet, milky tea, we set off to establish the shooting line.

In any game drive, the positioning of the guns is critical to success. It is essential to do the positioning as unobtrusively as possible so as not to alarm any game that may be in the area and which would clear off if alarmed. Uncle Rama did it himself, making sure not only that each person was positioned strategically to cover a given expanse of ground, but that each person's 'territory' overlapped the boundary of his neighbor but was still at a safe distance from him. This way, the two guns would have a fair chance of spotting an animal between them, but would not accidentally shoot each other.

As I mentioned earlier, this is hilly country with steep climbs and deep valleys and ravines. Positioning all the guns means to walk the entire line and in the growing heat of the day, it's no picnic. The 'Brain-fever' bird and the always present cicadas were the only accompaniment as we were all sworn to silence on the pain of death. Once all were in place, and Uncle Rama was also back in his own station at the end of the line, he gave the signal and the beat started.

It is almost impossible to describe the excitement of waiting. First there is silence. There is no sign that anything is happening at all. Then slowly as some time passes, you start hearing the beaters. These are men who walk along towards you in a widely spaced line, simply talking to each other loudly, throwing stones into any likely looking thicket to raise any animal which may be hiding in it and occasionally shouting, especially if they wanted to alert the guns to anything special. The idea is to get the animals to move but not to scare them too much, otherwise they would come to the guns too fast leading to missed shots of worse still, wounded animals. The excitement is palpable and is the essence of the experience of being a 'gun' in a beat.

My own station was in the middle of a thick Ber (Ziziphus mauritiana) bush, very thorny and very uncomfortable even though some space had been cleared for me to stand in the center. Directly in front, facing a slope going down into the valley before me, a small section of the bush had been cut out so that I would have a clear field of fire. Yet to anyone looking at the bush from outside, I would be invisible. In this position, I stood, silently ignoring the flies and the dribbling rivulets of sweat going down my neck. It is important to remember that it is movement that attracts attention and makes one visible. If you are still and your body outline is broken up by the surroundings then you can be almost invisible even to anyone looking directly at you. But the moment you even blink an eye, you will become visible. I knew this very well and so stood very still listening to the sounds of the beaters.

His instincts were right. His uneasiness justified. He stood up and scented the air and could faintly smell man. The breeze was blowing to him from the lake below so he could scent them. He could also hear them talking to one another. He remembered an earlier instance a few years ago when he was not yet in his prime, when he was in such a situation. As he tried to flee from the men on that occasion, he almost came in the way of a tiger but strangely the tiger was more alarmed than he was and didn't show the slightest interest in him. Then he heard loud bangs behind him and to one side, and he ran for his life. He had no idea what was happening but he was glad that he came out of that unscathed. Today once again, it seemed that it was something similar. Something that didn't bode well for him if he didn't get away. He was still not in a panic. But he was definitely fearful and extremely cautious. His senses were all at peak alert, trying to sense the slightest movement before him or scent on the breeze as he purposefully climbed up the hillside to get to the path he knew would take him down the other side to safety.

And then it happened! I saw some movement directly opposite me, coming up the slope. First, I saw the tips of his antlers, then the head and neck and then the full deep chested body of a full-grown Sambar stag, alarmed but not scared, looking over his shoulder occasionally as he climbed the hill, coming directly at me. I can never describe the majesty of his progress. He looked like the king he was, fearing nothing except the tiger and of course man. He knew that danger was behind him and knew how to get away. The wind was blowing up from the lake from him in my direction, so he had no idea how close he was to me. He was huge and as he came up the hill, he grew bigger in my eyes. In such a situation when you are either facing grave danger or high excitement, you live in the moment. Adrenalin is coursing through your veins and heightens all sensation. You see in vivid color, you smell all the variety of smells coming your way on the breeze and you feel the heart pounding in your breast and hear your blood racing in your ears.

I could smell him, the rank smell of cattle. He had been rolling in mud and his coat was caked in it. But what I noticed was the deep raking marks of tiger claws on his withers. This was a stag who'd had a close brush with death. I wondered how he got away. But he had and here he was, facing death again but without the slightest idea about it. He had a big head of antlers, the ideal trophy for me right in the beginning of the drive. What phenomenal good fortune for me, I thought.

My gun was already at port and to gently bring it to my shoulder and my cheek to the stock was a matter of an instant and I was looking at the throat of the Sambar through the open sights. I took in the slack of the trigger and knew that if I just squeezed my grip one degree, this stag would become a trophy in my house. And that is when I discovered something about my own nature. I discovered that it was impossible for me to kill something as beautiful and majestic as this. I just stood there and looked, drinking in the sight of this fabulous animal coming up the slope, carrying his antlers as proudly as any king with his crown. When he came right to the top, I whistled. The change in his stance was magical. One instant he was looking backward concerned about the sounds of the beaters. Next instant, electrified, all his adrenaline pumping into his bloodstream, he honked in alarm and was gone in a flash.

That was effectively the end of the drive for me as I was no longer in a mood to hunt. I just sat and enjoyed the scenery and re-lived the experience of my Sambar again and again. To this day, I can see him walking up that slope, coming to the gun held by a boy who would not shoot. When we all collected after the drive to look at what the bag was, the beaters asked me about the Sambar which they had seen. Nobody was amused or impressed with my story of why I could not bring myself to shoot the animal. Uncle Rama kept silent in all the ribbing that I was getting. When the others had gone off, he came to me and said, "Yawar-baba, I am proud of you. What you did is true sportsmanship." Such were my teachers. The lesson to follow my heart, notwithstanding unpopularity, is something that I have never forgotten all my life.

Tiger conservation is more about humans

THERE IS A welcome awareness about the need to protect tigers in the wild and the wild places they live. Welcome even more because it comes now at a time when the tiger population in India (numbers are even more elusive and ephemeral than the tiger) has fallen from 100,000 in 1900's to less than 3000 today. Frankly, one needs to ask the question whether tigers in India can realistically be protected in the wild or whether one should look to a rescue plan rather than a protection plan.

Be that as it may I want to state here the major issues which have led to this situation and addressing and solving which is absolutely critical to protecting tigers. You will see that almost all of them have to do with people more than tigers. The two major issues are habitat destruction and the market for dead tigers.

1. **Habitat destruction**: This happens for two major reasons.
    a. Our tiger reserves (except in one or two cases) are surrounded by villages. They cook on wood fires and the forest provides the wood. Our forest protection laws prevent them from cutting live trees, so they ring bark trees and cut them when they dry. Or they partially cut the tree and wait for the next wind to drop it and then they have their firewood. Human ingenuity, fueled by hunger and real need does wonders.

b. Villagers have small fields in which they do marginal agriculture and grow food grains and vegetables for themselves as well as to make a small income. If they can cut a few forest trees in the adjacent forest and expand their land holding, it means free land and the wood from the cut trees as a bonus. It is amazing how many crimes become invisible when some of this largesse is wisely spread around.

c. The fields and their produce is precious. It needs protection. In the old days before electricity came to the villages, the villagers used to build high platforms in the fields and sit up all night periodically beating tin cans to drive away any straying grazers or wild boar. After electrification, things became easier as was perhaps intended but not in this way. Villagers now simply hook a naked wire to the electric pole or their irrigation pump connection and string it at ankle height along the boundary of their land. Anything that comes into contact with it, fries. That way they can have a peaceful night's sleep and perhaps a high protein meal the next day.

d. Villagers are poor, have cattle to graze but no money to pay for the fodder. They can't grow their own fodder and stall feed their cattle as they need their small fields to grow food grains. So they take their cattle into the forest to graze. Cattle eat the grass that otherwise prey species herbivores would have eaten. Cattle are cows, buffaloes and in many cases goats. This means that they feed on grass as well as leaves. Their dung of cows and buffaloes is carried out by the grazer as they dry it and use it as fuel, so it doesn't add to the organic matter on the forest floor. The urine and dung of goats is highly toxic to plant growth. Cattle also carry foot and mouth disease (what politicians have is foot in mouth) and rinderpest which is highly infectious and lethal especially on Gaur. Cattle grazing in tiger land is like waving an ice cream cone under my nose – hard to resist a bite. Then the tiger is labelled 'cattle lifter' (instead of 'cattle acceptor') and pays for his hunger with his life.

e.   Then there is the territory problem. Tigers are solitary territorial creatures who will fight to the death to defend their territories. If there is over crowding of sanctuaries, tiger populations decline. Given the huge tract of land an individual tiger needs, we simply don't have the kind of area to support increasing tiger populations. So relocation, captive breeding and new sanctuaries are all options that must be explored. Young tigers seeking to establish their own territories will travel. This exposes them to temptation (cattle killing) and to poachers. Animals adapt to changing situations but the tiger has far more difficulty than its much smaller cousin, the leopard. And the day will never come when traveling tigers will thumb rides on trucks on the highway.

2.   **Market for dead tigers**: The market for tiger bone powder, skin (not so much today) and body parts. Tiger bone powder is more expensive than gold, precious stones or any illegal

narcotic drug. It is easy to conceal and transport and easy to sell for those who have the contacts. Killing a tiger is easy. Poisoning is the most usual way. Then the rest follows. http://bit.ly/1PsPk3g National Geographic Tiger Temple, Thailand investigation. This is the natural result of the market for tiger products. For them the tiger is like a sheep in a farm. Or a chicken. You don't object when it is slaughtered and its body chopped up and sold. So why do you object if it is a tiger? A farm is a farm. What is on the farm is not the issue. It exists for profit. There is a market. So the trade will continue. That is the logic. Try beating that logic. The tiger in the wild is even better because it cost the seller nothing to raise and it still fetches the same money. The trade is not in skins any more. It is in meat, bone and body parts. Which means that hiding it is even easier.

Solution:

1. All people have to be removed from tiger sanctuaries. All villages must be relocated. Much more difficult option is temples inside sanctuaries as there is in Sariska. But without relocating, the temple traffic and all its attendant evils can't be controlled. The amount of plastic and garbage in Sariska all along the route to the temple and at the temple itself is incredible. I saw a Neelgai bull trying to get into an empty potato chips packet. I am sure he managed and then swallowed it and eventually died of obstruction of his intestine. Who cares?

2. Then we have to kill the trade. That is what funds poaching and makes it lucrative. As I said, tiger bone powder is more valuable than any precious metal, illegal drug or precious

stone. As long as that market remains, there is a price on the head of every tiger.

3. A time is coming soon when tigers will only be left in zoos. That is why captive breeding programs are important. And then reintroduction into the wild.

4. We need a combination of habitat conservation with very tough laws that are actually implemented, very tough policing with shoot to kill orders on poachers, liberal compensation paid instantly for every domestic animal that is PROVEN to have been killed by a tiger, education about conservation in every school and college and connection with forests built into the education of all our children.

5. I don't mean going to sanctuaries and zipping around in Gypsies – which if I had my way, I would totally stop – but actually walking in the bush, camping at night, sleeping under the sky, reading sign, photography and sketching, learning jungle lore. That is what builds a connection. Not the TIGER SHOW that happens in our sanctuaries – which is so embarrassing and idiotic that it is not funny at all. Twenty Gypsy vehicles, with people dropping out of the sides and a tigress walking nonchalantly past threading her way through all the chattering monkeys. Ugh!! If I were a tiger, I would commit suicide.

6. It will be conservationists, hopefully supported by a live media which has a chance of making an impact on tiger conservation. With habitat destruction and the trade in tiger parts, it is a losing battle. Local people must see how protecting tigers will put food on their table and money in their pockets. Only then will they be allies.

7. All of the above can be tackled but the pressure of population and vote banks is the biggest threat. Politicians

always want to appease their voters. They have to. You can't
blame them. That is their bread, butter and lots of jam. They
need to be educated that the survival of the tiger is vital
because with them will survive the forests and show them
how that will still get them elected. Don't ask me how. But
that is critical. Until we can show a direct link, they will not
support the tiger against their vote bank. Sadly, tigers don't
vote. People do.

I hope that by the time our politicians can be educated, there
will still be tigers left to save. Indian forests without the tiger will
be like a body without a soul. Dead.

Devariya Taal

A journey in the Himalayas

WHEN WE THINK of trekking we think of walking long miles, climbing hills and watching nature in all its splendor. For me, trekking is all that. But even more important is the time alone which enables me to look within myself, gather my thoughts, revisit my dreams and discover myself.

Most recently I went on a trek in the foothills of the Kumaon Himalayas in Uttarakhand. I want to share that with you. I have just recovered from a series of three operations for hernia. Three because the first two failed, thanks to some incredibly incompetent surgery. However Indian culture being what it is I am none the richer for it. However, I was very keen to start walking again and to prove to myself that I had indeed recovered fully. As it happened I had an assignment with the SSB Academy, Gwaldam. The SSB – Sashastra Seema Bal is one of our border guarding forces that guards the Indo-Nepal border. I took that opportunity to go for a small trek after completing my assignment.

To get there, you take the train – Ranikhet Express – from Old Delhi station and get off early next morning at Katgodam. I was met by the SSB driver and gunner who had been detailed to receive me. The driver is an old friend from Manipur, all of 4 ½ feet tall, who gives the most brilliant salute accompanied by, "Jai

Hind Shaaar!!". It makes you feel 10 feet tall to be greeted like that. I did the best salute that I could manage and returned the greeting, "Jai Hind", standing to attention. Mercifully I have had a lot of practice in these things and managed to do a reasonable job.

From Gwaldam we drove to Ranikhet. This takes about 3 ½ hours and can be done by bus or car. The road is very good and goes along a river for the most part. All along the riverside there are tall Thorny Dadap (Macaranga Indica) trees in bloom. The flower is blood red and the tree completely devoid of leaves. The flower has nectar in its center and attracts a lot of birds. Truly a beautiful sight.

Almost midway we come to Bhimtaal which is a lovely lake bordered by lots of trees. The road runs along the edge of the lake and if you have the time you could stop at one of the tea shops for a break. If you leave Katgodam as soon as you arrive then by the time you reach Bhimtaal, the sun would be at an angle where the little wavelets turn to silver. What strikes me the most, every time I have done this drive, is the silence. Coming from the noise of big cities, this is a most welcome change. That and the clean pure air.

Having had your tea, you start again up the road and about 2 hours later you enter the town of Ranikhet. This is a district headquarters and the seat of local government. It is also the Regimental HQ of the Kumaon Regiment. The Regimental Museum is well worth a visit and is open to the public. The Kumaon Regiment has an interesting history. The Kumaon

Regiment was raised in Hyderabad on March 1st 1922 by Nawab Salabat Jah Bahadur who was a brother of the Nizam of Hyderabad. It was called the 19th Hyderabad Rifles. Later it was named The Kumaon Regiment and is headquartered in Ranikhet in Uttarakhand.

Some comments about this regiment which will interest Hyderabadi readers:

http://www.bharat-rakshak.com/LAND-FORCES/Army/Regiments/Kumaon.html

• Comments: The Kumaonis had been in British military service since the early 19th Century. As part of the North Indian class, who had joined the military of the East India Company's forces, the Kumaonis had moved to other states in search of military service. Thus they formed part of the Hyderabad Contingent, which was raised, trained and led by British officers under Henry Russel, but paid by the Nizam of Hyderabad. In 1857, in keeping with the class based composition of the infantry, the Regiment comprised Rajputs, Jats and Muslims. After the Great War, some Kumaoni battalions were raised separately, but the Hyderabadis continued and fought with distinction in the World War. In 1945, the Hyderabadis became the Kumaon Regiment. When the Naga Regiment and the Kumaon Scouts were raised, they came under the aegis of the Kumaon Regiment.

Ranikhet is an Army town and large parts of it are Cantonment and belong to the Army. Consequently it has not gone the route of most Indian towns and cities and still has open areas, parks, a golf course and old bungalows. Some of these are now being taken over by the new Uttarakhand State Government and being converted into hotels presumably one step before being knocked down to build apartment blocks in our standard architectural style called Modern Indian Horrible. But if you go quickly you will still see this beautiful town before it goes the way of others.

Having had a good breakfast in Ranikhet you proceed further up the road and about an hour or so later you come to Kasauli. This is the first clear sight of the Himalayan snow peaks that you should be able to see. You can see the peaks from Ranikhet as well on a clear day but the Kasauli sighting is much better. Certainly, a good bit of luck is needed in this matter as the Himalayas are both shy and hospitable. Shy to show themselves and hospitable to any passing cloud that wants a shoulder to cry on. So, for a great deal of the time they are hidden by cloud masses. It is only when it gets cold that the clouds do what clouds do and you can see the snow peaks. Kasauli also has a tea shop that belongs to the Uttarakhand Tea Corporation which serves some excellent high grown teas. You can also buy some to take back, but let me warn you that the price is not cheap. Having had our fill of the Himalayan views and tea we then proceeded further up the road to our final destination, Gwaldam.

Gwaldam is at an elevation of about 7000 feet above MSL (mean sea level) and can be very cold. Especially when it rains. The

Himalayan peaks that you can see from there are Trishul and Nanda Ghutti (not to be confused with Nanda Devi though it is the same range). And they seem to be in your front yard. If you were a crow and flew towards them, they are not more than 9 – 10 km from the Deodar tree in Gwaldam from which you would take flight. But since you are not a crow you will have to be content with taking photographs. Gwaldam has lots of Deodars and Pines. The sound of the wind in them is like the sound of the waves of the ocean. Interspersed among them are the signature plants of this elevation, Rhododendrons (Buraans as the Kumaonis call them). These are short trees, maybe 10-12 feet tall and when in bloom, entirely covered with flowers. The flower looks like a large rose and has fleshy petals that are edible. They make a juice from them which they claim is beneficial for people with hypertension. I have seen Rhododendrons in four colors, rose pink, blood red, powder pink and white. It is an amazing sight in March – April to see entire forests of these trees, as if splashed with multi-colored paint. A total abundance of color. You can't be blamed if you wake up one morning and look out of your tent and start to imagine that you had died the previous night and have now woken up in heaven. Misty valleys, grassy meadows mowed smooth by herds of sheep, forests of Rhododendrons, sunlit glades in which you can see Muntjac and Monal Pheasent.

Amazing bird, the Monal. The colors of the Monal can't be described. The closest I can come is to say that it appears that there is an electric light inside the bird because it seems to glow from within. The colors are fluorescent and kaleidoscopic. It shimmers in the early morning light and watches you warily over the shoulder as it moves away. And then with its typical whistle it flies heavily off. I always thought the Peacock as the ultimate in beauty until I saw the Monal. A pity that thanks to indiscriminate hunting their numbers are sadly reduced.

In March you will also see some compacted, snow in the shadows where the light of the sun does not reach it. Little streams flow from unexpected places and meander through the meadows and make little waterfalls off the rocks here and there. The water is ice cold and good to drink. Not too many places left in this country where you can drink the water straight from a stream and live to tell the tale. But I am living proof that provided the stream was in the hills of Uttarakhand you will be none the worse for your drink.

From Gwaldam we took the road to Karanprayag. The road winds along the Pinder river which is on your right at the bottom of the ravine.

The Pinder is ice cold and fast flowing, sometimes loaded with mud if there has been any rain in the upper reaches. It has very inviting sand banks on most bends but it is dangerous to camp on them on account of the danger of flash floods. The Pinder also has some excellent trout fishing. And if you are among those who either don't or can't fish, you can buy the trout from the several little road-side shops if you reach them early enough in the morning. The shops also sell rice and curry. The curry will take the top of your head off to let out the steam, if you, the unwary fall upon it with open mouth. The anti-dote is not water but plain rice or curds (yogurt) which the shop will also sell you.

Having got some 2 kilos of freshly caught trout, we proceeded on our way to Karanprayag. This is where the Pinder meets the Alaknanda. Together the two flow as one until they come to Rudraprayag where they are joined by the Mandakini. The three then flow along together until Devprayag where they meet the Gangotri which comes from Gangotri glacier and together they flow down to the Bay of Bengal. Only, now the river is called the Ganga. From Karanprayag we drove along the road climbing and winding along the Alaknanda until we came to the village called Sari.

These roads with the mountain on one side and a sheer drop on the other are maintained by the Border Roads Organization, a wing of the Indian Army and known for their expertise in maintaining mountain roads. They do such an excellent job that they are justly famous all over this region. Were it not for them, the 6-hour journey from Gwaldam to Sari would have been many hours longer.

Sari is the end of the road. At Sari you leave your transport and first sit in one of the tea shops to drink some tea. You would have noticed that tea and sitting in the tea shop are important rituals of this trail. Indeed, they are. For they have less to do with the business of drinking tea than with meeting local people, getting news and negotiating for porters and mules. All done in mountain time. So, don't allow your city urgency to get the better of you. Drink the tea, watch the view and let the villagers make the beginning.

"Would you like to go up to Devariya Taal?" one will ask.

Resist the urge to reply, "No. I have come to live with you in Sari for the rest of my life." And say, "Yes. Is it possible?"

"Yes of course it is." And then the negotiation for rates of porters and mules begins. You can carry your own packs of course, but since we hadn't had time to acclimatize we decided to play it safe and carry only ourselves and leave the rest to the mules. Now, don't get me wrong. The idea of negotiation is to keep up the tradition and so that everyone has fun all around. The hill people don't cheat you. What they ask is nothing more than what they deserve. And seeing that for you this is entertainment while for them it is a living, I would never dream of giving them a pie less than what they ask for and then give them a big tip. Yet we have to negotiate. For negotiation is a tradition that must not be treated lightly.

So little Prakash says, when asked for the rate for his mule, "Aat saw rupya sahib (800 rupees Sir)." And I say, "Yaar tere khachchar ka kiraya poocha. Usko khareedna nahin hai. (My friend, I asked to hire your mule, not to buy it.)." And we all have a good laugh and the negotiation is on its way. Eventually we agree to a rate that is a few rupees less so that his face is saved by showing how magnanimous he was to reduce his price but not too much. And my face is saved to show how magnanimous I am that I gave him almost what he asked for. And of course, you would never just give the asked for price. That way you would show what a fool you were and nobody would have any fun negotiating. When we returned the next day, Prakash got a thousand rupees from me, being his original price and my tip. But that is also understood and expected.

Once you have finished negotiating, then you simply leave all your bags with the mule keeper and start the climb. The hill people ate scrupulously honest and you need have no fear of losing anything from your pack. So, you start off.

Much to your disgust, as you are about midway up the hill, panting for breath and asking yourself why on earth you had been so foolish as to imagine that you could do this trek, along would come Prakash and his mules, almost running up the steep climb and pass by you with a smile on their collective faces. No, you can't kill Prakash. It is illegal. But then, as you take the next turn in the path, there he is, standing by with a brass lota (urn) filled with ice cold stream water, offering it to you, "Paani piyenge sahib?" What lovely people!!

From Sari village to the top of the hill is 2000 feet straight up. If it was any steeper it would be a wall and not a hill. The path winds along like a demented snake and so you end up walking a little over 2 kilometers. The Forest Department in its kindness has paved the path with stones. This makes it uneven and a very hard surface underfoot. And so it is now harder to climb than it would have been on the soft soil forest pathway that it has replaced. But that is entirely in keeping with all government projects. Tell me one, which actually makes life easier. On you climb.

Every time you believe you are dying, just stop and look back. Stone shingle roofs of the village houses, terraced fields growing wheat. You always thought that green was one color. Look at the terraces below you and you will realize that green is a thousand colors. You always thought that the wind was invisible. Look at the crop growing in the terraces and you will see the wind as it brushes the ears of wheat and bends them symmetrically in its passing.

Reflect that every terrace has been built by hand, each stone bordering it, collected individually and placed skillfully so that it remains in place through the heavy monsoon and snowfall. Reflect that the soil in the terrace field has been carried there and added to every year. Each field represents the work of many generations, handed down from one to the other. Think about the hydraulic engineers who have managed to direct the flow of a small stream so cleverly that it irrigates many terraces and not a single drop of water is allowed to go waste. And then remind yourself that none of these engineers ever went to school. They learnt engineering in the school of life where the prize is survival and failure is starvation.

As you look and think and breathe the clean, cold air, your tiredness falls away and you get invigorated with new energy and once again you turn around and begin climbing. Now as you climb, look about yourself. Try to count the thousands of Rhododendron blooms. My friend Mr. G. C. Sah, Head of Outdoor Education at the SSB Academy, Gwaldam who was with us, calls them, 'Ro Dho climb on' – Cry, wash your tears, but climb on. Truly beauty can wash away exhaustion. As you climb, do pick a few petals of the Rhododendron flower and chew on them. They have a slightly sour tangy taste and are very pleasant to eat. Since you are not in any hurry and walk at a normal pace that is not too taxing you can do the whole climb in about 2 hours.

When you reach the final lip be prepared to have your breath taken away. For as you climb over the top, you suddenly see Devariya Taal spread before you. Set like a jewel in the middle of what you may take to be a golf course. So closely has the grass been cropped by the sheep which graze there. The lake is green with algae as the water is still and has no flow. It is really a collection of rainwater and snow-melt and perhaps has a spring or two at the bottom. So in the summer when the sun is bright, algae has a field day and the whole lake becomes a dark green in color. Devariya Taal has a lot of fish, mainly carp, as far as I could make out. Some fairly large.

Fishing is permitted from the bank and there is no boat, so you can only catch some very small fry which are really not worth catching. So after catching two, to prove that we could catch them, we threw them back in the water. You can pitch your camp on the high bank at the back of Devariya Taal from where you get a good view of the Himalayan peak called ChowKhamba. On a clear day when the sun is just right, Chowkhamba gets reflected in the waters of Devariya Taal, truly a magnificent sight.

When we reached the top, our support staff has already pitched camp and had a hot cup of tea ready for us. Most welcome indeed and heavily laced with sugar, gave us a much-needed energy boost. The sun was already starting its journey to the bottom of the mountain. In the mountain the light goes very rapidly, so it is a good idea to ensure that all you need to do is done before it gets dark. Wandering around on steep mountainsides in the dark is a good way to meet a quick end.

Since we did not need to actually do anything ourselves, we just sat and watched the sun go down.

Watching the mountain as the sun sets is an experience in itself. The snow changes color with the light. First it is white as it reflects rays that are stronger and more direct. It shines and shimmers and you have to shut your eyes in tribute to its brilliance. Then as the angle of the sun changes and it starts going down the snow changes color to pink, to orange to the beginning of a grey that eventually turns dark. All in a matter of minutes. But interestingly it never completely turns dark. There is always some ambient light from the stars or moon that keeps the snow lighted just a little. Such are the delights of the mountains.

I can write a great deal more about the whole businesses of trekking but this will do for now. All that remains is to light the camp fire, tell stories while you cook your food. And then eat and sleep. Night comes early in the mountains, as does day. So, eat well and sleep well. For tomorrow is another day.

Yala, Leopard Paradise

He had killed the buffalo late the previous night. The dark was his friend. Thanks to the reflectors in his eyes, he could see as clearly in starlight as we can see in bright daylight. If he could have read a book, he would have, reclining on a massive tree branch overhanging a pathway. As the light faded and night set in, he was on his favorite perch, only his tail hanging over the side, announcing his location. He had climbed the tree earlier in the evening to give the Langur sentinels and their friends, the Axis (Cheetal) deer to sound their alarm calls and eventually tire of it when they couldn't see him any longer in the gathering darkness. The sun goes down rapidly in the tropics and Yala National Park, where he lives is in the far south of Sri Lanka. He is a leopard (Panthera Pardus kotiya). A big male, full grown and at the peak of his powers. The Sri Lankan Leopard is a subspecies native to Sri Lanka that was first described in 1956 by the Sri Lankan zoologist Deraniyagala. In 2008, the Sri Lankan Leopard was listed as Endangered on the IUCN Red List.

But he didn't know all this. All he knew is that he was the top predator in the forest and, so he could roam where he wished and take whatever suited his fancy, at will. There are no larger predators in Sri Lanka unlike India and Africa where leopards live in fear of tigers and lions. In Yala and other national parks of Sri Lanka, the leopard is king, and this shows in their behavior. Yala is the only place where I have seen leopards stalking along a road in broad daylight. And wonder of wonders, I saw a full grown young male lying under a bush, with several jeeps full of tourists ogling at him from just a few feet away. He made no sign of leaving nor did he show even the slightest nervousness. The only cat which does that in India is the tiger and in Africa, the lion. Though the African leopard (Panthera Pardus Pardus) is a larger animal, it is very secretive and almost totally nocturnal. He is far too fearful of lions and rightly so. So also, the Indian leopard (Panthera pardus fusca), is wary of the tiger which would kill it if it could.

Sri Lankan leopards grow bigger than their Indian cousins because of their top predator status and because there is abundant game in Yala. Not only are there huge herds of Axis deer (Cheetal) but feral water buffalo and wild boar. In addition, it appears that villagers are permitted to graze their buffalos in Yala and I saw a great many of them as well, quite at peace with those that appeared to be wild. I think this is a very bad idea as invariably this invites man-animal conflict and the loser is always the animal. In this case, the already endangered leopard.

To return to our story he made his kill as the buffalo, a fully grown but young female was returning to her herd. As she passed under his tree, he landed on her back and bit into the back of her neck, severing her spine. The buffalo bellowed in pain and fear, took a few lurching steps forward trying to dislodge him from her back but in vain. By then the massive jaws with their powerful bite did their work and the canines sank through skin and gristle and severed the spine. The buffalo collapsed in its tracks and the leopard, lithely leaped off and immediately grabbed her throat in the classic killing stance of the leopard, cutting off air and possibly severing the carotids. In this case, this was not necessary as the buffalo's spine had been severed and so it was going nowhere. It is interesting to speculate on the killing technique which is like that of the tiger when it tackles Gaur; the massive wild ox of India. Tigers also leap on to the backs of Gaur, preferring younger bulls or cows and bite into the back of the neck to sever the spine. That way they incapacitate an animal that is otherwise more than able to kill the tiger, being far heavier and having a pair of lethal horns.

After killing his prey, the leopard fed on it until he was full and then dragged it behind a large Lantana bush to hide it from Jackals. There are no vultures in Sri Lanka. Neither are there any Hyena or Wolves. So, Jackals are the only ones likely to try to steal a bit of meat from the kills. Other leopards are a threat but in this case, he was so massive and powerful that he didn't really expect another of his species to take any chances with him. Leaving the kill behind the bush, he climbed an old Banyan (Ficus Religiosa) nearby and stretched out on his favorite branch to sleep off his meal. Early the next morning, just as the sun was starting to show on the horizon and the Sri Lankan Jungle Fowl with its splash of bright yellow on its comb, started calling, to be answered by the Peafowl roosting on the topmost branch of a dead tree with its feet in the flood waters of the river, he walked down the trunk and leaped down the last few feet to return to his kill to take some more mouthfuls of the, by now, reeking meat.

As he was tugging at an especially tasty bit, we drove up on the jungle road going past his cache. I saw the leg of the buffalo move which meant that the killer was on his kill. We stopped and waited but there was no sign of him. Then my friend Ifham

Raji, a wonderful professional photographer from Colombo, who very kindly accompanied us and gave me lessons in the field, decided to call. He can imitate the call of a female leopard calling its young. Until that moment, we didn't know what would come out. All we knew was that there was a leopard kill and we had come to see if we could get a look at the one who made the kill, if possible.

As soon as Ifham called, a guttural, woof; he came out from behind the bush in one short rush. He stood there looking for his mother whose voice he had heard. Then he walked towards our jeep and about twenty meters from us, he turned to his right and walked a few steps and lay down. Then he rolled over, as if he was playing, his tail high in the air. He sat up and looked at us directly. Then he decided he didn't like being fooled and walked away. That was the last we saw of him and though he must have returned to the kill later, we never saw him again. The sight of his massive head and shoulders, his fluid majestic walk, his stand looking at us in total confidence and then his playful rolls on the ground as he would have done as a cub, playing with his mother and siblings, etched into my memory. Was he remembering his own childhood? Did the call remind him of his childhood? Who knows?

All I know is that I got some amazing photos and lived through an experience that can have no parallel. This is the gift of the wild places, which one can only experience. Indeed, I can write about them and you can read what I write and see the pictures. But I can't for the life of me, express the excitement of the moment when for me time stood still; I stopped breathing until I had to gasp for breath as if rising out of the depth of the sea to the surface and forgot all about Aperture and ISO while taking my photos. But as a person learning photography, I can tell you that I would rather spoil a thousand photographs, than lose the excitement of the moment when you first see a big cat. The leopard is my favorite but don't tell the tigers that. They are elusive enough when I try to find them.

Respect earns respect

There are ocean people and others who are mountain people; and yet others who are city people. I, am of the forest people. Wildlife, open spaces, mountains and forests have always been a very significant influence in my life. There is an instant connection that I find with forests. And every once in a while, I rejuvenate myself by spending time in forests, listening to them, watching animals, and simply being.

The sounds of the forest herald the passing of time and the arrival of the night and day. And they vary from place to place. In the Anamallais, the rain forests of the Western Ghats, there are no peacocks, who are usually the first heralds of the coming night in the forests of central India. In the Anamallais, the first heralds are Jungle Fowl roosters. They start calling (as they do at the approach of the morning) as they go to roost. They make sure that they are perched high up out of harm's way well before it becomes fully dark. I must add this piece here. I was in the Anamallais in April, 2013 and to my intense surprise found peacocks thriving. This is a clear indicator that the amount of rainfall has decreased, for peacocks don't survive in high rainfall areas like the rain forests of the Western Ghats. I asked around and everyone agreed that this was the first time in living memory that anyone had seen peacocks in the Anamallais. Alarming news.

To go back to our story, after the Jungle Fowl roosters come the calls of the Lion Tailed Macaques and the Langur sentinels who boom out their announcement to the world. These calls are not alarm calls. They are just to let their troops know that it is time to settle down for the night. Closer at hand you can hear the 'Brrrrr!!' of the Night Jar as it settles in the middle of a path or in a clearing and suddenly darts up to catch the unwary moth. As the sky darkens, you hear the hoot of the newly awake owl (many different species) as it ruffles its feathers and gets ready to take off on its nocturnal hunt. Then there is silence for a while. As the night progresses and if you are lucky, you can suddenly hear the 'Dhank! Dhank!' alarm call of the Sambhar as it sights a Tiger or Leopard out on the prowl. Sometimes you will hear the sawing growl of the leopard. The sawing call of the leopard is for courtship. Usually the cats go on silently so as not to alarm their prey unduly.

In the winters late in the night you will hear the moaning roar of the tigress, during which she literally bends down and booms off the earth and the sound of which travels for many miles. Sometimes the tigress calls continuously for hours. At other times you will hear her on and off. At all times it is a thrilling sound guaranteed to raise the hair on the back of your neck. Tigers don't have a breeding season as such but I seem to recall hearing them mostly in the winter in the Aravallies. The primordial memories of the hunter and the hunted travel through the genes. As do their responses.

In the Anamallais, which is prime elephant country you can also hear the king of the forest as the whole clan moves along, grazing. Branches breaking, sometimes a tree pushed over so that the hungry pachyderm can get at the succulent leaves at the top, which he loves. The rumbling of their bellies and the snorting of mothers and aunts as they try to keep the calves in line. Calves squealing and the sounds of playful trumpeting as they sometimes engage in mock battles. Sometimes you can hear the long moaning rumble of the matriarch as she calls to others who only she knows about. This low frequency sound carries for many miles and is answered by other family groups in the vicinity. As they are all happily going about their business of feeding and playing, the wind changes and they get a scent of you sitting in the tree. And there is change as if by magic. The noisy group of huge animals instantly falls silent and moves through the forest like shadows. It seems amazing to those who have not had the good fortune of encountering elephants in the wild and have not seen how silently and quickly they can move in the thick forest. Not a leaf crackles. Not a branch snaps underfoot. When the elephant wants to move silently he becomes a ghost. And he is gone.

On one occasion I was walking along a forest path in Manamboli in the Anamallais when I smelt elephants. So, I simply got off the path and into the forest, not more than a few meters away, hidden in the foliage. As I stood there, waiting for them, the whole herd emerged around the corner, all headed to the river from which I had just come. Believe me, they knew I was there and knew I was coming down that path far better than I could ever sense their movement. There was the matriarch who led the herd, some other females, young calves and a couple of bulls. But all of them simply walked past me without any comment. The one thing you learn in the forest is that respect gets respect. You respect the animals and they respect you and leave you alone. You are not in the slightest danger unless you do something silly like trying to scare them, or run away in fright or in some cases if you are completely unaware of their presence and blunder into them. Otherwise a normal wild animal will never attack you unprovoked. Animals are far better mannered than humans.

On another occasion, I was on my Royal Enfield motorcycle with a bag of cash on the petrol tank. The tradition in the tea gardens where I was the Manager is that workers are paid in cash directly by the Manager. This is considered the respectful way to do it. Workers would all line up outside the Muster on payday and come in when their name was called and greet you and take the money and thank you. For each one you returned the greeting, paid the money, waited for them to count it, returned their thanks and then called out the next name. Sounds tedious but it is a brilliant way to learn people's names and to build relationships. To do this, we used to take the cash out of the safe in the Estate Office, count it – amounting sometimes to half a million rupees – and take it to the Divisional Muster for the payment. It is a mark of the safety of the times that we could do all this without any 'security'. I can't recall a single instant when anyone was ever held up and the cash stolen.

To return to my story of respecting animals, on this day I was going to the Candura Division in Lower Sheikalmudi Estate and decided to take a shortcut through our coffee plantation which bordered the forest. This was one of my favorite routes as in the short drive of perhaps five kilometers I could be sure to see several species of animals or birds. There were Grey Hornbills, Malabar Squirrels, Lion Tailed Macaques (which the locals called

Yel-Tee-Yam). In season, Green Imperial Pigeons beautifully camouflaged and usually on the topmost branches of the figs that attract them when they start fruiting. The fig is the best tree to attract birds. So there I was, gently riding my bike, looking around to see what I could spot; the finely tuned engine just turning over almost silent when I turned a corner and right in the middle of the road was a very large Gaur bull. Lone bulls usually mean trouble. And when that is a Gaur, standing six feet plus at the shoulder and weighing half a ton or more, it is generally not good news. But what could I do? I was on my bike on a narrow forest road with a steep bank on one side and a drop on the other. The only way I could even turn the bike would have been to get off and do many back and forth pushing and pulling. Anyone who has ridden a Royal Enfield can understand what I was facing. Trying all these gymnastics on a jungle track, balancing half a million rupees in a duffel bag on the tank with a bull Gaur as your audience is not my idea of fun.

So, I did what any sensible person who knows animals would do. Nothing. I did nothing. I just stopped, kept the engine idling and looked at him. He looked at me for what felt like a couple of hours but was perhaps ten seconds, snorted and with great dignity, moved aside to let me pass. He didn't run away. He didn't even go far from the road. He just moved aside. I knew what he was telling me and so I put the bike in gear and also with dignity, unhurried, rode past him. He could have ambushed me or attacked me as I passed him or after, but I knew he wouldn't do it. He knew he didn't need to. And here I am remembering him and our meeting.

The final story of this dispatch is to do with Wild Dogs, the dreaded Dhole. Anyone who has read Rudyard Kipling will remember the Dhole. Romantic notions apart, they are a top predator and hunt in packs. The Dhole is a very handsome animal with a reddish-brown coat and a black-tipped tail. They can't bark and communicate in whistles. Their favorite prey in the Anamallais is Sambhar. The individual dog can't possibly kill the Sambhar which is far bigger and heavier but the pack working together is an unbeatable team. They literally run the animal to the ground and when you are talking about thick forests on steep mountains, that doesn't take too long. Then they hamstring it and when it drops, start eating it alive. Nature is sometimes very ugly. But there it is. An ecologist friend said to me that the Sambhar at the end is probably so pumped full of adrenalin that it doesn't feel a thing, but I am not so sure because sometimes they take a very long time to die, mostly due to loss of blood. Meanwhile they have the Dhole tearing into them and eating their living flesh. Definitely not a sight for anyone.

My story has to do with one day when one of my workers came racing to me and between panting breaths told me that a pack of Dhole had taken down a pregnant Sambhar doe and were eating her, very close to the worker's quarters which we called Labour Lines. There is a lot of military terminology in the tea gardens, a memory of the first British planters who were military officers who came to India after being de-mobbed. I followed the man to the site. The doe was lying on her side in the middle of a clearing, almost all of it covered by sheet rock, in the middle of a valley surrounded on two sides by tea and on one side by the forest. She had been chased out of the forest and seemed to have come there to take refuge with people who Dhole avoid but before she could reach the quarters, she had collapsed. The pack was in a feeding frenzy, making excited yelping sounds. There were fifteen animals in the pack which is quite large for a single pack but when food is plentiful they tend to have large litters.

I watched from the edge of the valley for a bit and thought I could see the doe still kicking. I decided to put the poor animal out of its misery and drew my knife and walked down into the valley. The Dhole saw me coming, whistled to each other and moved off a few meters away and sat down in a semi-circle watching me. I walked up the doe and realized that she was dead. The kicking I had seen, was the result of the Dhole pulling at her carcass. They had ripped open her belly and eaten her unborn fetus, udders and were feeding on the stomach contents from which they get minerals. Definitely not a pretty sight. I made sure the Sambhar doe was dead and turned around and retraced my steps. The Dhole watched me go and returned to their kill. They never threatened me or made any attempt to attack. They knew I was not going to steal their prize. I don't know what else they thought. But I do know that when you respect animals, they respect you.

Wilpattu...Land of the lakes

He came with a lizard in his beak. A choice tidbit, most appreciated. But only if you're a Sri Lanka Grey Hornbill (Ocyceros gingalensis). The female lays up to four white eggs in a tree hole blocked off during incubation with a cement made of mud, droppings and fruit pulp. There is only one narrow aperture, barely wide enough for the male to transfer food to the mother and chicks. These birds usually live in pairs or small flocks consisting of up to five birds (2 adults and 2-3 juveniles). They are omnivores observed consuming berries, fruits, insects and small lizards. It feeds mostly on figs, although occasionally it eats small rodents, reptiles and insects.

We, my friend Ifham Raji and I were parked in our open Toyota Hilux safari vehicle, our cameras mounted on sand bags placed on the roof of the cab and focused on the hole in the tree which was the Hornbill nest. We could see the beak of the female from time to time as she threw out the waste from her nest, ensuring that it remained clean.

It was early morning and the forest was filled with birdsong. A Shama (White-rumped shama - Copsychus malabaricus) alighted on a twig facing me, scarcely five feet away and gave me a personal recital of his song. I wanted to photograph him but decided only to let my memory do the job for fear of scaring him away with my movement. The Shama has a black head, a brown waistcoat and a black tailcoat with two long tail feathers.

On the back is emblazoned his white shield on which he hasn't inscribed his coat of arms yet. The white shield on the back is very striking. But above all this, what impressed me was his attitude. Confidence, curiosity, friendliness. He came, he saw, he sang and he conquered my heart.

Meanwhile the male Hornbill came with his delicacy but looked extremely suspicious and skittish. I wondered whether we were the cause of his alarm or anything else, until I saw two other Hornbills, fully grown juveniles, that flew in as if they'd been lying in wait for him. One, which I think was the male, dive-bombed him to try to make him drop his catch. That was fairly easily taken care of by the simple action of swallowing it. When this tactic didn't work after trying it several times, the male gave up and went off into the forest. The female decided that the best way was to appeal to whatever nobility existed in the heart of her father and simply begged. She did that so pathetically and effectively that he eventually coughed up something for her. I say "father" because that's who he was. These two were his fully grown millennial chicks from a previous brood, who know what human millennials worked out only in this generation. That it's easier to live off your parents than to work for your own living. Hornbill youngsters do that for a year or more after they are fully fledged until the parents finally kick them out altogether. The interaction was fabulous to watch.

This is my greatest pleasure in bird photography; watching interaction as birds afford you an opportunity that mammals and reptiles don't. Birds go about their lives as if you don't exist and allow you a glimpse into their lives that's a privilege which pays the patient who value their time. You may be surprised to see the use of the phrase, "value their time", in a context different from the usual. We imagine that our frenetic lifestyle is worthwhile and that the best use of time is to cram as much into it as possible with no thought about what we get as a result. I believe that the best use of time is to consider the result in whatever we propose to do with it and then spend the time only if the result warrants it. Time is not money. Time is far more valuable than money. Money can be earned, lost but replaced. Time is free, can be lost but never replaced. That's why I'm very careful with my time and consider sitting for six hours watching a Hornbill father take care of his mate, while avoiding the raids of his children, one of the most beneficial uses of my time. That's how long it took us to get some decent photographs.

So now there was the father, finally having got rid of his pesky brood, ready to feed his mate. But with what, I wondered. Because he had swallowed the lizard to save it from being eaten. Sounds oxymoronic but there it was. So I watched. He looked all around. Called a few times to assure his mate that he still loved her. His raucous call that can be music only to a female Hornbill's ears. He flew from perch to perch all around the nest-hole to assure himself from every angle that the coast was clear. Then he landed on the vertical trunk of the tree, on the lip of the nest-hole. Then I lo'ed and beheld, to my amazement, the lizard emerge. And after it, a large green beetle, a large black beetle, a large grey caterpillar, and one after another a series of black berries (not the phone, real ones). Not having been a Hornbill ever, in my career, nor privy to his loading sequence, I can't say if everything came out as it was ingested. But the lizard was last in, first out. Then he was off.

The second trip was a repeat of the first. We wait and wait. The Shama takes pity on us and returns to sing us another song. Then the juveniles return to check out if dad is back with food. The male chick is chased out of another part of the forest by a highly aggressive and territorial Golden Oriole. The GO is one sixth or less in size but has ten times his courage. So throwing all dignity to the wind, the Hornbill chick makes haste with the GO in hot pursuit. All he had to do was to stand and say, "Okay, do your worst." And the Oriole would have come face to face with his limitations. But this is a world of deception, even for birds and noise counts more than action.

I sensed something behind us. I had been listening to some movement in the forest with an occasional branch breaking and dry leaves gently rustling. Could be jungle fowl or monkeys. But as I turned around, I saw the biggest cow elephant that I've ever seen in this part of the world. Sri Lankan elephants are the biggest of Asian elephants and this one was proof. She came out of the forest like a shadow, in total silence. She turned and looked at us in the safari jeep, barely 20 meters from her. Then she turned and walked away with elephantine dignity that only elephants can muster. No aggression, no posturing. Someone who knows herself and her own power and has no need to demonstrate it to anyone. Someone who is content even to let those intruding into her space, to do so without protest, as long as they are respectful. Big question in my mind is what she was doing alone. Where was her family? We saw her twice more, both times alone. I wonder what that story is.

Meanwhile the Hornbill returned, this time, regurgitating a series of red berries, one after another and passing them to his mate through the hole in the wall. It was amazing to see the precise nature of the sequence where he would bring out one at a time, run it up his long beak, and very delicately drop it into the nest. I didn't see him actually feeding his mate nor did I see her take the fruit from his beak. But it all went into the nest-hole. A Barking Deer cautiously made his way out of the forest on my right and hurriedly crossed the open patch of the road and entered the undergrowth on my left. My dilemma was whether to photograph him and risk disturbing the Hornbill. But he solved my dilemma by taking off again on his never ending quest to keep his spouse happy. Never saw anyone work so hard at this. Reminded me of the picture I see every morning in my mirror.

Yeah! I know. Where's the scene of all this action? Wilpattu National Park, Sri Lanka. A world heritage site and the oldest national park in the country. Flat land, very sandy, with very large trees and lots of lakes. Villu is Tamil for lake and Pattu means ten. There are more than forty in the park but ten large ones, thus the name. The Sri Lankan Department of Wildlife Conservation (much better name than Forest Department, because it speaks of their focus), has built bungalows (rather grand name for cottages) on the banks of some lakes. They location makes up for the lack of maintenance and resultant challenges is staying in them. The one we stayed in had no door handles or latches. So at night I had to push an extremely heavy bed against the door to keep out any potentially unwelcome visitors. The same was the case with the bathroom with the added joy that the floor tiles squelched and squirted water, ever time you stepped on them. But the joy of a cold shower at the end of a hot, humid day compensated for the squelchy floor tiles. The bungalows have solar power but no fans or plug points. So no charging of phones. There is no signal anyway so the death of the phone goes unmourned. But the impending demise of camera batteries is another matter. At any rate this adds to the excitement of trying to conserve battery power and shooting wisely.

Also no fans means that hot humid days are exquisite torture. But all you need to do, to forget the discomfort is to look out from the veranda at the lake before you. Brown grass in the foreground, getting greener as it nears the water. Lush green grass closer to the water, then reeds and then the inviting blue of the lake itself. Do not yield to the invitation to jump in. Jump into the squelchy shower instead because in Wilpattu and Yala, every puddle has its resident croc. Not the shoes but the real ones. Ranging in size from cute and cuddly to enormous maneaters, which probably never ate a man and so would be doubly anxious to try one out. You'll also see lots of birds on the Villus (lakes, remember?).

On our Villu, in one afternoon, I saw a pair of Wooly-necked storks walking purposefully looking at the ground. An Adjutant Crane (a very ugly bird) walking with whatever dignity it could muster while being harassed and chased away by a pair of Red-wattled Lapwings, screeching their alarm call, Did-you-do-it, Did-you-do-it? The Adjutant hadn't but his reputation of eating eggs and chicks is enough to pronounce him guilty in the eyes of the Lapwings and they didn't want him in the vicinity. Then there was a pair of Malabar Giant Hornbills crossing the lake, their characteristic flight, their signature. There were perhaps thirty or forty butterflies congregating on a patch of moisture. They attracted the attention of a Green Bee Eater, which decided that he was not bound by his name and had no objection to eating butterflies also. After the fourth swooping flight and the fourth butterfly which became history, they got the message and dispersed. But not before a fifth one was picked through the air. GBE's are such graceful flyers and such attractive birds.

What strikes me yet again is how alive the forest is. As we were sitting in the jeep waiting for the Hornbill to turn up, I could hear an absolute orchestra of bird song. I could identify five or six but there were at least another dozen that I didn't recognize. Yet all this is not noise or cacophony just like the infinite variety of color has nothing that's mismatched.

After we got the last shot, we headed back for our bungalow. As we came to yet another lake, this one covered in white lotus flowers, I spotted a pair of Eurasian Thick-knees (Eurasian Stone Curlew) doing what they do best; just being. I recalled having spotted them many times in several countries but always simply being; doing nothing. What's their purpose in life, I asked myself. They do nothing. Not even search for food; at least whenever I was watching. Ifham tells me, "I know a lot of people in the cities who run around all day but do nothing. These birds are doing it better because they're doing it without expending any energy." And he's right, isn't he? There was an Egret which was flirting with a baby crocodile. Until the little croc lunged forward. The Egret did some inspired gymnastics and got away otherwise the little croc would have had a bird brain for dinner.

The sun had set. We finished our dinner. I'm sitting with my cup of tea after which I intend to go to bed. A Cheetal (Axis deer) sounds an alarm, the Langur sentinel takes up the call, then a Sambar bells his call. Now I can be sure that the leopard is on the prowl. Leopards are the apex predator in Sri Lanka and so the Sri Lankan leopard (Panthera Pardus Kotiya) is the largest of its species. He behaves the way a tiger behaves in the Indian forest and so if you want to see leopards, Sri Lanka is the place. Since they have no enemies, they walk around during the day and are very relaxed when you spot them either dozing on a tree branch or on the ground, in the shade of a tree. You'd never see that in India or Africa where leopards must always be on the lookout for tigers and lions, who will kill them as soon as look at them. But in Sri Lanka they have nothing to fear and so are much easier to spot.

I hope the leopard will come around the bungalow in the night and I get to hear his sawing grunts. The night is alive with its own sounds. Nightjars announcing that they're on duty. The Brown Fish Owl calling his mate. Two Spotted Owlets discussing hunting strategy. Langurs murmuring after hearing the far sentinel announcing that the leopard's on the move.

Life goes on. The struggle continues. Some win. Some lose. For some, it is only fun. He also serves who only bears witness.